UBUNTU

Life Coping Skills
from Africa

UBUNTU
Life Coping Skills from Africa

Johann Broodryk

KNO RES
PUBLISHING

2006

First published in 2006
ISBN 1-86922-143-5

Published by Knowres Publishing (Pty) Ltd
P O Box 3954
Randburg
2125
Republic of South Africa

Tel: (011) 880-8540
Fax: (011) 880-8700/9829
E-mail: mail@knowres.co.za
Website: www.kr.co.za

Printed and bound by: Creda Communications, Johannesburg
Typesetting, layout and design: Stephani Smith, (083) 678-3936
Editing and proofreading: Elsa Crous, getitedited@mweb.co.za
Cover sketch: Marle van Pletsen
Cover design: Carike Meiring, 43 Degrees Design, carike@43degrees.co.za

DEDICATION

To my friend, the poet Uhuru:

Keep the word on the streets!

CONTENTS

About the author _____ v

Acknowledgements _____ vii

Testimonial _____ xi

Introduction _____ xv

1. THE WORLD VIEW OF UBUNTU _____ 1
    Ubuntu life lessons and skills_____ 1
    Historical background_____ 4
    The ancient Holy Belief of Maat (Ubuntu) _____ 6
    The influence of Maat on religion _____ 9
    Poem: Ubuntu call for help_____ 12
    Layout of this book _____ 13

2. MEANING AND PERCEPTIONS OF THE
    UBUNTU WORLD VIEW _____ 17
    Definitions and perceptions of Ubuntu _____ 17
    Ubuntu in other African languages _____ 23
    The prominence of Ubuntu _____ 24
    Ubuntu values _____ 26
    Case study: Captives of taxi violence _____ 29

3. THE VALUE OF HUMANNESS _____ 31
    Introduction _____ 31
    Human rights _____ 34
    Tolerance _____ 35
    Understanding _____ 38

Peace _____ 39

Humanity _____ 40

Case study: Robben Island experience _____ 40

4. THE VALUE OF CARING_____ 43

Introduction _____ 43

Caring and children_____ 46

Empathy _____ 47

Sympathy _____ 48

Helpfulness_____ 49

Charity _____ 50

Friendliness _____ 50

Case study: The echo of life_____ 51

5. THE VALUE OF SHARING _____ 55

Introduction _____ 55

Sharing and family _____ 58

Giving unconditionally _____ 59

Redistribution and greed_____ 60

Open-handedness _____ 60

Case study: The greedy poultry farmer_____ 61

6. THE VALUE OF RESPECT _____ 63

Introduction _____ 63

Commitment_____ 67

Dignity _____ 67

Obedience_____ 68

Order _____ 69

Norms _____ 70

Religiosity_____ 71

Appreciation _____ 72

Consideration _____ 73

Children's rights _____ 74

Case study: The lobola issue _____ 75

7. THE VALUE OF COMPASSION _____ 77
    Introduction _____ 77
    Cultural differences as regards compassion _____ 79
    Love _____ 81
    Cohesion _____ 82
    Informality _____ 83
    Forgiveness _____ 83
    Spontaneity _____ 84
    Kindness _____ 85
    Case study: Application of compassionate values _____ 86

8. THE PRACTICAL LIVING OF UBUNTU VALUES _____ 87
    Traditional life _____ 87
    Modern living _____ 90
    Life during the apartheid era _____ 94
    Moral regeneration _____ 97
    Case study: Application of Ubuntu in practical life _____ 99

9. UBUNTU SELF-MOTIVATION _____ 101
    Introduction _____ 101
    Self-motivation methodology _____ 105
    Identifying the problematic issue _____ 106
    Formulating a personal vision _____ 109
    Defining a personal mission _____ 109
    Using a personal ONPO-analysis _____ 110
    Developing a personal action plan _____ 112
    Personal action programme _____ 113

Exercise: Alcoholic-to-be _____ 113

Case study: Story of an artist _____ 114

10. THE UBUNTU COUNSELLING PROCESS _____ 117

Introduction _____ 117

Analogy "pitseng" African pot_____ 117

"Pitseng" (African three-legged pot) methology _____ 119

Counselling through Ubuntu _____ 120

The role of counsellor_____ 121

11. UBUNTU SKILLS_____ 127

A word of caution _____ 127

The Ubuntu personality _____ 129

Ubuntu skills _____ 131

Ubuntu: Philosophy of happiness _____ 157

Case study: Surviving an earthquake _____ 160

12 THE WISDOM OF UBUNTU _____ 163

Introduction _____ 163

To ponder on _____ 163

Personal exercise: Living Ubuntu values _____ 165

Bibliography _____ 169

Index _____ 175

Glossary _____ 179

Abbreviations _____ 182

Addendum: Training Programme _____ 183

ABOUT THE AUTHOR

Dr Johann Broodryk was the first person to obtain a doctorate on the ancient African philosophy and world view of Ubuntu, with a D Litt thesis entitled: "Ubuntuism as a world view to order society". Awarded by the Department of Philosophy at the University of South Africa, Broodryk's thesis was dedicated to Dr Nelson Mandela, former President of South Africa, and a man who embodies the Ubuntu personality.

Broodryk was also part of the Research Unit for African Philosophy, at the University of South Africa. He was mentored by several acknowledged African intellectuals on the subject of Ubuntu (people whom he acknowledges in this book) and did empirical research in different remote areas of Africa, from rural KwaZulu-Natal, up north to Kenya.

Broodryk established the Ubuntu School of Philosophy - a training and research enterprise and consultancy based in Tshwane, South Africa.

He currently teaches Ubuntu life coping skills, advises employers on Ubuntu management skills, and trains counsellors in the methodology of Ubuntu philosophical counselling.

Broodryk has appeared on various television and radio programmes on the subject of Ubuntu. He has also contributed academic as well as popular articles on Ubuntu and delivered a variety of papers on this subject at conferences and workshops.

Training enquiries: Ubuntu School of Philosophy
P.O. Box 95240, Waterkloof, 0145, Tshwane
Republic of South Africa
Tel +27 12 993-3163
e-mail johann@ubunturesearch.co.za
www.ubunturesearch.co.za

ACKNOWLEDGEMENTS

I wish to acknowledge my African mentors who taught me about Ubuntu - amongst them, people whose works I have studied intensively.

Walter Sisulu, former Vice-President of the ANC and a man who was my first mentor on Ubuntu

Dr Kgalushi (Drake) Koka, African Study Programme and Karaites Institute of Afrikology, Jo'burg (Afrika was originally used by Africans when they referred to Africa due to Arabic influence; the colonial name Johannesburg has officially been renamed as Jo'burg).

Prof Lesiba Joe Teffo, Department of Philosophy, University of the North, Limpopo Province

Prof Joe Diescho, Department of Political Science, University of Pretoria, Tshwane

Dr Joe Ndaba, Department of Philosophy, University of KwaZulu-Natal

Prof Augustine Shutte, Department of Philosophy, University of the Western Cape

Prof Magobe Ramose, Department of Philosophy, University of South Africa

Prof Lovemore Mbigi, Business Studies, Cida University, Johannesburg

Archbishop Desmond Tutu, Chairperson of the Truth and Reconciliation Commission in South Africa and Nobel Peace Prize winner, whom I met by chance while doing research in Kenya

Mfuniselwa John Bhengu, Ubuntu Academy, Durban, KwaZulu-Natal

Dr Mathole Motshekga, Kara Heritage Institute and former Premier of Gauteng Province

Prof Gail Presbey, previously of the Department of Philosophy, University of Nairobi, Kenya, and presently teaching African Philosophy in the USA

Ruel Khoza, former Executive Chairperson of Escom, Jo'burg

Uhuru Phalafala, poet and Rasta philosopher, Jo'burg

Prof Danie Prinsloo, former Head of Department, Philosophy, UNISA

Dr Dirk Louw, Department of Philosophy, University of the North

I wish to extend a special word of humble gratitude to the honourable Dr Nelson Mandela, former President of the Republic of South Africa.

I dedicated my D. Litt thesis, the theme of which was *Ubuntuism as a world view to order society*, to Dr Mandela for personifying the ideal qualities of the Ubuntu personality, and he signed the original copy of the thesis.

I also refer numerous times to Mandela's autobiography, *Long Walk to Freedom* in this book.

I wish to express my sincere gratitude to all of the above mentors, as well as to the ordinary individuals who taught me valuable lessons on Ubuntu. These teachings helped me learn about and appreciate Africa with all its wisdom on life coping skills.

Apart from research of an academic nature, I also learnt about Ubuntu from the people at grassroots level, through empirical research in various rural areas of Africa.

As a world view Ubuntu has tremendous potential to influence society globally, and make it a more human, caring and sharing open society. Ubuntu encompasses what and how you think, speak and act, what you value and how you arrive at your destination in life.

Ubuntu is about the African art of being a true human being through other true human beings. In the words of the IsiZulu proverb: Umuntu ngumuntu ngabantu.

Dr Johann Broodryk
Author
August 2006

TESTIMONIAL

Ubuntu (humanness), as a philosophical concept, is as old as the beginning of the creation of the human race, and originated from the four categories of created things: Humans, anmates/inanimates, modalities, and localities.

Man was declared human as soon as the element of divine goodness was instilled in him. This divine element, that transformed man (matter) into a human being, was nothing but a humanness, uBuntu that manifested the likeness and image of God in each individual person of the human race. It was the spark of life that transformed man into a living soul and made him different from the rest of the created beings. That is, man immediately contained the main constituents of the wholeness of life, namely:

$$Ka = Spirit$$
$$Ba = Soul$$
$$Chat = Body$$
$$(KabaChat).$$

It endowed man, who was nothing but matter with consciousness, with intelligence, wisdom, love and compassion, reason, understanding and creativity.

This gave man power of dominion over all creation.

The concept (uBuntu) was there from ancient times and has never ceased to exist within the circle of the human race up to modern times. It was mentioned in doctrines of well-known ancient philosophers who, in turn, were scholars of the Hermetic Philosophy, Theology and Science, which were based on the LOGOS (Creative word) doctrine taught by African priests of Kemet (Egypt). For instance Pythagoras, who studied African philosophy for 22 years at the University of Heliopolis under two Egyptian high priests namely Sochts and Onuiphis, mentions the Inner value and dignity of the human personality which is nothing but a humanness instilled in man. This teaching was based on the hermetic doctrine of macro-microcosmic theory of creative emanations.

The above theory held that human beings, like the Cosmic Monad (Atum/Creator-God) first evolved into Ntu (Nut)-Ra (two in one); secondly into Triad (three-in-one = Mundu) and lastly into a fourfold principle – which is the fountainhead of nature and primal image of the Gods – according to Thoth-hermes – who was referred to as the personification of the mind of God.

He (Thoth-Hermes, 10400 BC) also taught that the human personality, Bundu/uBundu consists of the triad and the principle comprising, in figures, 3+4=7 - that explains why figure 7 is the most important figure in the life of a human being. It is the symbol of a Perfect man.

Plato, who was the pupil of pythagoras, followed in the footsteps of his master and in those of the two Egyptian priests who tutored him for 12 years, in the study of the macro-microcosmic theory of creative emanations.

The doctrine stated, amongst other things, that God (Supreme Good), did not only endow man with his goodness, but also, equally inseminated this divine element into all human beings which is the main theme carried out in the research work of Dr Broodryk.

A remarkable feature of the above scholars is the length of time taken to study and master African philosophical concepts.

It is alleged that two French anthropologists, Marcel Griaule and Germane Dieteren, took 16 years to achieve their goal, namely, the study and full understanding of the culture of the Dogan people of Mali, their religion and philosophy and totality of their life (humanness). Their mission was accomplished after the elders of the double village Ogol, along with the most important hogons (priests) of Sanga, held a conference and decided to reveal the more esoteric aspects of their religion (or theosophy). It is only then that they were given privilege and assistance to delve into the intricasies of the word (at value simple knowledge), the word on the side, the word from behind - and only 16 years later did the elders decide that they were ready to receive this knowledge - and the clear word (the abstract and esoteric knowledge).

Remarkably, this is almost the scenario that Dr Broodryk had to go through. The only difference with the abovementioned scholars of African philosophy is that Dr Johann Broodryk took only six years to study, investigate and comprehend the concept of and praxis of the uBuntu philosophy.

Like his predecessors in the field of philosophy, Greek scholars in Egypt, the two French anthropologists, and others in the quest knowledge, Dr Broodryk mixed and discussed with African common masses, even during times when it was legally undesirable for whites to mix (socially) with Africans.

We need to congratulate Dr Broodryk since he has successfully dealt with the subject as a philosophical concept, showing us how it can be applied in almost all sectors of life.

He dealt with definitions of uBuntu as given by various writers with whom he consulted, and also explained, how uBuntu can be applied in practice in areas like...

➢ self-management
➢ values: case studies of Ubuntu
➢ Ubuntu life skills.

The words and style are presented in a manner that can be understood by all members of the community, which makes the research suitable for consumption by both adults and youths.

This leads me to make a strong suggestion that his research be prescribed in the Education Department in the discipline Ubuntu as a blueprint for new world order and harmonious co-existence in our democratic South Africa.

Ntate Kgalushi Koka
Director: Karaites Institute of Afrikology
Jo'burg
South Africa

Itroduction

Ubuntu is the ancient African world view and philosophy of humanness.

All people can learn from this very respected and sacred philosophy, which explains how Africans cope with life through spontaneous behaviour and a happy approach to life.

The author of this book, Dr Johann Broodryk, was the first person to obtain a doctorate on the topic of Ubuntu. He obtained this qualification from the Department of Philosophy, University of South Africa.

In this book, Broodryk exposes the life lessons of Ubuntu (which allegedly originated 1 500 years before the discovery of the Ten Commandments), as a means of coping with life successfully – based on guidelines which emanate from the African tradition.

The outcome of practising these life skills is a less stressed and happier experience of life. These treasured basic lessons and skills for happier living are explored as acknowledged African intellectuals and ordinary people provided them.

Broodryk believes that if Africa has something to offer the global society, it is indeed the human-based life coping skills of Ubuntu.

This book makes essential reading for people seeking alternative solutions to enjoy a happy and qualitative life.

It is also recommended for those with an interest in African culture, anthropology, philosophy, political science, sociology, education, business and counselling.

Ubuntu is being taught in all schools in Gauteng Province, South Africa. Ubuntu forms the moral basis of the national education values in South Africa. Education departments throughout the continent of Africa, are investigating the possibility of introducing Ubuntu as compulsory subject in all schools.

Both old and young will benefit from the ancient life coping lessons of Africa.

Dr Johann Broodryk
UBUNTU SCHOOL OF PHILOSOPHY
TSHWANE: SOUTH AFRICA

The World View of Ubuntu 1

"The great powers of the world may have done wonders in giving the world an industrial and military look, but the great still has to come from Africa — giving the world a more human face."

Steve Biko (1978:46)

UBUNTU LIFE LESSONS AND SKILLS

Imagine an old man entertaining children, who are sitting in a semi-circle around him. He's telling them a story with a moral bite: A life-coping lesson in typical African style.

His story is most probably aimed at teaching the younger generation some of the values embedded in the ancient African world view of Ubuntu (African humanness), as was once the custom.

These Ubuntu life-coping lessons are nothing new: They have been handed down from generation to generation through centuries – as is still the custom today. In the past this was done in an oral way, through the dramatic and entertaining art of storytelling.

The internationally acclaimed African philosopher Credo Mutwa sets the scene (1966:vii) for the stories old men and women would tell boys and girls, seated with open mouths around a spark-wreathed fire at night, in the middle of their village in a dark forest or on the aloe-scented plains of Africa...

Mutwa teaches: "Under the gaze of the laughing stars the Old One sits, his kaross (blanket) wrapped around his age-blasted shoulders, staring with dreamy eyes at the semi-circle of eager, expectant faces before him – faces of those who have taken but a few steps along the dark and uncertain footpaths called Life – faces of the ones as yet oblivious to the pain of life's bitter scourges – faces as yet unmarked by furrows of bitterness, ill-health and anger – the fresh, open faces of... children.

The fire dances in the middle of the round, clay fireplace like a virgin revelling in the simple joy of being alive. It devours the dry twigs and logs that a little girl is constantly feeding it, leaving nothing but glowing ashes. It mocks the silent sky with a redly luminous column of smoke against its starry face and by sending up short-lived stars of its own.

Suddenly the Old One feels a great burden on his shoulders – a heavy responsibility towards the young ones sitting so expectantly around him. Suddenly there is a visible sag to his thin, aged shoulders. He sighs – a harsh, rasping sound – and clears his throat, spitting and blowing his nose into the fire, as his father and his father's father did before him. And he begins the story – the old, old story which he knows he must repeat as he heard it so long ago, without changing, adding or subtracting a single word..."

It is a story in the tradition of Ubuntu, an ancient life-coping lesson from Africa.

Life lessons and life-coping lessons are basically closely related: Both refer to advice and wisdom on life issues. Life skills and life-coping lessons are also applicable to all aspects of life, but the emphasis of the latter is on actually implementing the advice of life lessons.

Usually a distinction is made between hard skills and soft skills. "Hard" skills refer to solid, tangible and measurable skills, and "soft" skills are regarded as being amorphous, intangible and more difficult to measure.

In this book the concept of life-coping skills will be utilised as life lessons which can be implemented in practical terms.

The author aims to present values which direct behaviour, to suggest how one can implement values as practical life-coping skills for a happier life, and give an overview of the outcomes of a happy Ubuntu lifestyle.

Life skills are described (Van der Wal, 2005:4) as the basic developmental blocks of human existence. These "enable all of us to love and do productive work, or to empower a person to use life skills as tools to enhance his/her well-being."

The Ubuntu approach to life skills is aimed at appreciating and enjoying life in all its manifestations as you live the primary values of humanness, caring, sharing, respect and compassion.

Other general concepts like business skills, counselling, HIV/AIDS assistance and prevention, human rights, success, work ethic, volunteering, effective communication, conflict management and related issues can be connected with the basic values of Ubuntu.

If Ubuntu is implemented in a more global manner, it will pave the way for more harmonious and meaningful human co-existence.

The ultimate aim of implementing Ubuntu globally may be the creation of a new, moral world order, which manifests in the establishment of more humanised societies, and more caring, happy, yet disciplined individuals.

The whole world could use a massive moral injection of Ubuntu.

Historical Background

According to Koka (2002:4) Africa had an enormous influence on intellectual development globally.

Many years before the story of Adam and Eve in the garden of Eden, and many years before the birth of Moses (1316 BC), Africans in Egypt, as well as other nations of the Nile and the great lakes of the region, were already engaging their creative genius in subjects like mathematics, religion, astronomy, geology, medicine, theology, philosophy, law, architecture, engineering, agriculture, rhetoric, physical training, music, art, grammar, logic and liberal arts.

In referring to "The role of Africa in the development of the world" it is alleged (Nemavhandu, 2002:2) that the Greeks' plagiarism of African (Egyptian) science, philosophy and religion can be proved beyond any reasonable doubt.

According to this source, that which Western (white) historians claim contributed to the rise of Western civilisation, is an example of such plagiarism.

Egypt was the main centre of education in the ancient world, and black Egyptian priests were the tutors of various Greek and Western scholars. Black Africans also established the world's first known universities. Pythagoras and Euclid, well-known Western academics, obtained their knowledge from Egypt's "Sacred Mystery Schools" and it would constitute academic fraud to falsely credit them with their academic achievements. These schools were the first universities known to man and they had branches all over the world, including China.

The temple-university at Luxor housed an elite faculty of priest-professors and catered to some 80 000 students at all grade levels. Temples were at the centre of religion, politics and education.

A number of well-known Biblical figures, scientists, philosophers and theologians also attended this Grand lodge for their initiation, professional and academic qualifications. The lodge became the envy of many nations. It was the only Lodge (university) of great and advanced learning in the ancient world.

> **Egypt had world-famous schools of learning and great men and women never considered themselves educated unless they had attended the Egyptian School of Learning, the Grand Lodge of Luxor (Waart), which was built by Pharaoh Amonithes III on the banks of the Nile River in the ancient city of Thebes.**

Minor lodges were also established all over the world and it was through them that the teaching of African systems of education spread and influenced world thinking.

African culture was regarded as being highly developed in the ancient world. It gripped the minds of scholars, priests and kings. Egypt was like an amphitheatre where the art of creation was enacted.

It is therefore not surprising that some claim all world civilisations – on all continents – began with black Africans.

If Eurocentric historians argue that Europe gave civilisation to Africa, it is – according to Nemavhandu (ibid:5) – a complete perversion of the truth: "The first civilised Europeans were the Greeks, who were chiefly civilised by the Africans of the Nile Valley. The Greeks transmitted this culture to the Romans, who finally lost it, bringing on a dark age of 500 years.

Civilisation was restored to Europe when another group of Africans, the Moors, brought this dark age to an end. During the Golden Age of

Islam, the Moorish Empire was the most advocated state in the world. Cordova was the most wonderful city of the 10th century: The streets were well paved, with raised sidewalks for pedestrians. Public baths numbered in the hundreds, at a time "when cleanliness in Christian Europe was regarded as a sin".

Moorish monarchs dwelt in splendid places, while the crowned heads of England, France and Germany lived in big barns without windows and chimneys, and only a hole in the roof for the emission of smoke.

Africa also shaped world thought and action with noble principles based on the attributes of Maat (Ubuntu).

Maat (or Ma'at) is an ancient Kemetic (Egyptian) belief which explains the key elements of human perfection (Lesole, 2002:6).

THE ANCIENT HOLY BELIEF OF MAAT (UBUNTU)

The holy belief of Netchar Maat was assoc iated (Koka, op cit:10) with the seven cardinal virtues, or the keys to human perfectibility: Truth, justice, propriety, harmony, balance, reciprocity and order.

The seven virtues and the 42 Admonitions of Maat were guidelines for correct moral behaviour. These virtues form the basis for understanding Ubuntu, and can be applied to all levels of life.

The Admonitions of Maat were allegedly written approximately 1 500 years before the Biblical Ten Commandments were discovered.

The ancient 42 Admonitions of Maat, as translated from Arabic into English, are as follows:

1. I have not done iniquity
2. I have not robbed with violence
3. I have not stolen
4. I have done no murder, I have done no harm
5. I have not defrauded offerings
6. I have not diminished obligations
7. I have not plundered the Netchar
8. I have not spoken lies
9. I have not snatched away food
10. I have not caused pain
11. I have not committed fornication
12. I have not caused shedding of tears
13. I have not dealt deceitfully
14. I have not transgressed
15. I have not acted guilefully
16. I have not laid waste the ploughed land
17. I have not been an eavesdropper
18. I have not set my lips in motion (against any man)
19. I have not been angry and wrathful except for a just cause
20. I have not defiled the wife of any man
21. I have not defiled the wife of any man (Note: this appears to be a duplication)
22. I have not polluted myself
23. I have not caused terror
24. I have not transgressed
25. I have not burned with rage
26. I have not stopped my ears against the words of Right and Truth
27. I have not worked grief

28. I have not acted with insolence

29. I have not stirred up strife

30. I have not judged hastily

31. I have not been an eavesdropper (Note: this appears to be a duplication)

32. I have not multiplied words exceedingly

33. I have not done either harm or ill

34. I have never cursed the king

35. I have never fouled the water

36. I have not spoken scornfully

37. I have never cursed the Netchar

38. I have not stolen (Note: this appears to be a duplication)

39. I have not defrauded the offerings of the Netchar

40. I have not plundered the offerings to the blessed dead

41. I have not filched the food of the infant, neither have I sinned against the Netchar of my native tow, and

42. I have not slaughtered with evil intent the cattle of the Netchar.

According to belief the Ten Commandments were deduced from the above Admonitions of Maat, as follows (number of the corresponding Admonition of Maat appears in brackets, unless it is uncertain or unclear which admonition it corresponds to):

COMMANDMENTS	MAAT NUMBERS
I am the Lord thy God. Thou shalt have no other gods before me	**41**
Thou shalt not make unto thee any graven image	**unclear**

COMMANDMENTS	MAAT NUMBERS
Thou shalt not take the name of the Lord thy God in vain	7, 37, 41
Remember the Sabbath day, and keep it holy	unclear
Honor thy father and mother	1, 12, 28
Thou shalt not kill	4
Thou shalt not commit adultery	11, 20, 21
Thou shalt not steal	2, 3, 5, 6, 7, 9, 39, 40
Thou shalt not bear false witness against thy neigbour	8, 13, 18, 29
Thou shalt not covet thy neighbour's house or wife	13, 20, 21, 29, 33

THE INFLUENCE OF MAAT ON RELIGION

In Africa the Islamic and Christian faiths are predominant. The theological simplicity of the Islamic religion, which was founded by the prophet Muhammed (570-632), is probably best captured in its fundamental profession that there is no god but God, and Muhammad is His prophet.

This notion was confronted with the concepts and dialectic of Greek philosophy which in turn, as will be indicated, was influenced by the Maat principles and Christianity.

Christianity is one of the largest religions in the world, and is practised – especially in the Western world – on a massive scale.

People tend to base their life and world views on the faiths they believe in, and this tendency also influences followers of these two faiths.

Many who follow the prophecies and adhere to the wisdom of Jesus Christ will be surprised to note that He was allegedly educated by African mentors, and that the Christian Bible contains many Ubuntu messages. It is inevitable – if Jesus was in fact an African – that He would have been educated on the principles of Maat. If one reads the wisdom of Jesus's sayings and prophecies it becomes evident that they reflect elements of Maat (or original Ubuntu).

The Ten Commandments and the principles of Maat, as indicated earlier, basically teach similar messages when it comes to how to live.

The question also arises whether Jesus was in fact a black person. Not that the colour of your skin should be an issue when it comes to your religious beliefs, but traditionally the perception created in the Western world was that Jesus had been a white person.

It is claimed that various academic disciplines had their origins in Africa, and even that Jesus was not only a scholar from Africa, but also a propagandist of the cardinal values of Ubuntu, as set out above.

Koka (op cit:5) refers to the work *Aquarian Gospel of Jesus Christ*, Section XI, Chapters 47 and 48, pages 87 to 89, where the student days of Jesus in Africa, more specifically in Egypt, are extensively reported on. From this one can conclude that if this claim were indeed accurate, Jesus must have been in his early twenties at that stage of his life.

Extracts from this work read as follows:

"And Jesus came to Egypt land and all was well. He tarried not upon the coast, he went at once to Zoan, home of Elibu and Salomé, who five and twenty years before had taught his mother in their sacred school."

"And there was joy when he met them. When last the son of Mary saw these sacred groves he was a baby, and now a man grown strong by buffetings of every kind; a teacher, who had stirred the multitudes in many lands."

"And Jesus told the aged teachers all about his life; about his journeys in foreign lands..."

"And Jesus said... I pray you brothers, let me go into your dismal crypts; and I would pass the hardest of your tests. The master said: Take then the vow of secret brotherhood. And Jesus took the vow of secret brotherhood. Again the master spoke. He said: The greatest heights are gained by those who reach the greatest depths; and you shall reach the greatest depths..."

From this resource Koka could not find evidence that Jesus ever entered Europe or the West or indeed studied there, or that a single European had ever trained him. Instead there is abundant evidence that he entered Alkebu – Ian / Africa where he received training from indigenous African/black professors, scribes, theologians, metaphysicians, magicians, astronomers, mathematicians and scientists.

Nemavhandu (op cit:13) further claims that Jesus was in fact a black man (and a revolutionary fighter), and that it was the white man (Romans) who killed him. This is why the holy day on which Christians celebrate his death is referred to as "Good Friday". The name of the historical man was Jehoshua (or Jeshua), not Jesus. His original name was "Jehoshua Ben Pandira" which means "Jesus, son of the panther", and even the Bible refers to him as "the lion of the tribe of Jude".

This information may be regarded as shocking and controversial to some conventional Christians, but it is worth taking note of, as it is what certain African thinkers claim and believe.

It is obvious that Western Christians will most probably reject or challenge these claims since Christ is generally described as being of white descent.

However, the intention of the author is not to become involved in discussing the information as provided here, since it is not part of the scope or purpose of this book. It may, however, be an exciting exercise to do more research regarding these claims, and to discuss these claims in groups.

POEM:
UBUNTU CALL FOR HELP

There is some support for the idea that Ubuntu should be taught in both formal (educational) and informal institutions (families, extended families, churches, cultural bodies), in order to create a new moral world order. For that to happen, it would require broad-based support.

In this respect two Grade 7 pupils from the Ubuntu Centre outside Tshwane made this passionate (Infomax 3, 1994:10) plea to spur mankind into action:

UBUNTU IS CRYING FOR HELP

I am a word
which has been on earth for many years
I need you, mankind, to help me,
I cry day and night
but I don't find my answer
The only way you can help me
is by carrying me
in your hearts, your souls.
Please let me stick to you forever
and forever shall
I remain
in your hearts.

THE LAYOUT OF THIS BOOK

This book consists of twelve chapters.

CHAPTER 1: Here a distinction is made between life lessons and life-coping skills. It is argued that life lessons are transformed into life-coping skills once we implement them in our daily lives, in a practical way.

In a way lessons are the theory and life-coping skills are the practical tools with which to approach and build one's life.

The values of Ubuntu (as practical skills) are traced back to the ancient principles of the Holy Maat, followed by definitions of Ubuntu.

The concept of Ubuntu appears in some form in all the languages of Africa, and we will take a look at the relevant words used to describe it.

The primary and secondary values, as interpreted by the author after years of research in Africa, are provided.

CHAPTER 2: Here the author concentrates on the meaning and definitions of Ubuntu.

Examples are provided of how to interpret Ubuntu in daily life.

CHAPTER 3: This section investigates the value of humanness, with the focus on the "-ness" or spirit of Ubuntu.

Humanness is complemented by secondary values like tolerance, understanding, peace, humanity (which is different from humanness), and human rights. All these secondary values are discussed in the context of the Ubuntu world view.

CHAPTER 4: This section highlights the value of caring.

The concept of caring encompasses our attitudes towards children, as well as behaviours like being charitable, friendly, empathetic, sympathetic and helpful.

Caring is one of the main pillars of the Ubuntu construction.

CHAPTER 5: The focus here is on the value of sharing.

Sharing starts at home and is present in the life system of members of extended families and communities. Sharing means giving unconditionally, and in a spirit which is open to redistribution. It is closely related to open-handedness. Both the wealthy and the poor are expected to share what they have.

CHAPTER 6: This section touches on the value of respect.

Respect requires evidence of commitment, dignity, obedience, order, norms, appreciation, consideration and the upholding of the rights of the vulnerable (like children). Unless the world practises the basics of respect, its societies are indeed doomed.

CHAPTER 7: Here the need for compassion is stressed.

Compassion influences values like love, cohesion, informality, forgiveness, spontaneity and kindness.

In the modern world the need for compassion is becoming increasingly vital for ensuring the survival of human beings as people.

CHAPTER 8: Since it appears to be useless to theorise on values only, the possibility of living Ubuntu values in practice, is discussed here.

Ubuntu cultural concepts are direct outcomes of Ubuntu living in practice. These concepts are illustrated in both their traditional and modern contexts.

Reference is also made to traditional ways of authentic living in Africa.

Modern applications are discussed, as is the universal relevance of living according to the principles of Ubuntu – all cultures, religious and political beliefs, as well as world views can accommodate Ubuntu approaches. Ubuntu is African, but the values are inherently similar to those of people on all continents.

CHAPTER 9: This chapter explains Ubuntu self-motivation as an alternative to outside motivators. The principle here is that someone can motivate him or herself through self-analysis. The methodology for self-analysis as a self-help process, is provided (for example, how to identify problems).

This step is followed by the compilation of a personal vision and mission, by means of the Obstacles, Negatives, Positives and Outcomes (ONPO) analysis. It will be argued, and reasons will be provided as to why the ONPO analysis is more relevant when analysing human beings, than the conventional Strengths, Weaknesses, Opportunities and Threats (SWOT) analysis.

A case study provides an example of how to conduct an ONPO analysis.

CHAPTER 10: Here the author looks at counselling the Ubuntu way.

The value and advantages of positive thinking are crucial for cheerful survival – this is something which should be accommodated in the counselling process.

This process is compared to the process of preparing food in an African pot ("pitseng"). It covers all steps in the preparation process – up to and including the actual outcomes.

Counsellors are encouraged to become philosophers, listeners and questioners in Socratic and sangoma styles by refraining from providing advice, but rather by assisting others to arrive at their own solutions.

CHAPTER 11: This section covers the Ubuntu personality and relevant skills which result in the living of Ubuntu as a philosophy of happiness.

One important exercise is proposed to assist the reader in arriving at personal application possibilities aimed at coping with life.

CHAPTER 12: This deals with the ancient wisdom of Ubuntu made practical in the form of personal life values and coping skills.

Outcomes of this practical application are provided to explain how Ubuntu skills can benefit people of all cultures, when practising these life-coping skills.

Meaning and Perceptions of the Ubuntu World View [2]

"Umuntu ngamuntu ngbantu (I am a person through other persons)."

— *Kgalushi Drake Koka* (1996:3)

DEFINITIONS AND PERCEPTIONS OF UBUNTU

The late South African black consciousness leader Steve Biko (op cit:46) found that he was not comfortable with certain Western values and traditions which he regarded as foreign to Africans. He felt that these cultural components were not complementing the concept of Ubuntu as humanness.

This is also the essence of this book: To reflect on the importance of an Ubuntu human-centered world view and its relevant values, i.e. life-coping skills, in order to make this world a better and happier place for all to live in, and to learn what Africa has to offer all of us in this regard.

This is a plea for the creation of human environments characterised by less morbid attitudes and fewer stressful experiences, and more instances of sheer qualitative happiness.

In these human orientated environments one will observe qualitative happiness where there is less greed, imperialism, individualism, and more efforts to share in a spirit of collectiveness and communalism.

The challenge in reading this book, which may also be used as a manual for Ubuntu training and counselling, is for the learner to try to link the positive Ubuntu way of thinking and living to all events and approaches in life: As a world view Ubuntu encompasses everything the human mind can experience or think of.

A world view is described (Prinsloo, 1999:1) as a comprehensive view of reality providing a framework that serves as a conceptual scheme in terms of which a person tries to interpret reality (i.e. everything that is).

Examples of world views are materialism, idealism, animism and humanism. World views are distinguished from dogmas, theories, ideologies and theologies because these issues are limited in scope and were not intended to encompass all of reality.

Reality can have different meanings to different people: For Africans, reality consists of human relations (thus covering all aspects of human interaction).

The criteria for a world view are identified (Mutahhari, 1995:97) as follows: It

> ➤ can be deduced and proven
> ➤ gives meaning to life - it banishes from minds the idea that life is vain and futile, that all roads lead to vanity and nothingness
> ➤ gives rise to ideals, enthusiasm and aspirations
> ➤ has the power to sanction aims and goals
> ➤ promotes commitment and responsibility.

It will become clear in this book that Ubuntu adheres to all these characteristics of a world view. Ubuntu has already been "lived" by the vast majority of Africans throughout centuries, it provides meaning to life and is underpinned by wise lessons spilling over into precious coping skills; it encourages the development of personal and communal visions and missions, and its foundation is a way of life that is characterised by responsible commitments.

Generally, a world view influences life-coping skills. You can regard yourself as a manager of your own life by utilising the life-coping skills deduced from a world view, to make some sense of life.

Similarly, the material supplied in this book should be used as a foundation for understanding and learning life-coping lessons from Africa, which manifest in the actual "living" of practical Ubuntu values.

Definitions and perceptions are closely interlinked and they may not always be uncontroversial.

During the South African War against the British Empire in the early 1900s the British press, for example, described "Boer" women (white Afrikaner women) as fat, lazy, uncivilised, dirty and simply stupid. It was a British perception that existed at the time. It did not take into consideration the fact that these women were embroiled in a state of war, imprisoned in British concentration camps, and that clean facilities and other luxuries were simply not available.

Another example of a perception is that of the so-called tokolosh, which some people believe to be a real creature. They believe in the existence of the tokolosh which is apparently a small, devilish-looking animal with a reputation for raping loose women. The tokolosh, according to legend as well as the created perception, had a male sexual organ of about three feet long (and that was in its non-erect state!). As a result women took precautions against being raped by the tokolosh, by stacking bricks under their beds – by sleeping on a higher level, they would be out of reach of the little monster.

Defining Ubuntu is not an easy task due to the dilemma of different perceptions existing. The concept of humanness, for instance, is viewed differently by different cultures. It is acceptable practice in some countries to hunt animals with firearms merely for the pleasure of hunting, and hunters do not view this as an inhuman deed. In Africa this practice is regarded as grossly inhuman, since hunting is only excusable if it is for the purpose of feeding people.

In an address to youth leaders in Jo'burg, on 15 March 2002, Koka (2002:1) also referred to the dilemma of defining Ubuntu in exact terms due to the divergent perceptions attached to it. He compared the process of compiling a precise definition of Ubuntu to five blind men's search and subsequent attempts to explain what an elephant is.

Five blind men were invited to "see" an elephant. When they found one, they touched it. They returned from their mission elated – they were convinced they "knew" the elephant.

Sitting around the African fire that night (as is the custom when discussions are held and stories are told) each described the animal according to his tactile sensory experience, and each was adamant that his description of the elephant was definitive.

Here are their descriptions, based on their unique perceptions:

An elephant is like a wall, said the one who had touched the body
An elephant is like a stick, said the one who had touched the tail
An elephant is like a pillar, said the one who had touched the leg
An elephant is like a blanket, said the one who had touched the skin
An elephant is like a spear, said the one who had touched the tusk

They were all satisfied with their process of discovery and just as confident that they actually knew what an elephant was, not realising that their different versions were due to their individual, tactile experiences of different parts of the elephant.

Each of these perceptions gave rise to a unique definition or understanding of what an elephant is like. The question still remained:

Exactly what is an elephant?

The same argument can be applied in defining the concept of Ubuntu. What exactly does the term mean?

A definition of Ubuntu living is: "Every facet of African life is shaped to embrace Ubuntu as a process and philosophy which reflects the African heritage, traditions, culture, customs, beliefs, value systems and extended family structures" (Makhudu, 1993:40).

This definition emphasises the African-ness of Ubuntu, which has its origin in Africa. This does not exclude an appreciation for Ubuntu on the part of people living outside Africa. Eastern philosophies share many characteristics with Ubuntu - like the importance of families in raising children, as well as the phenomen on extended families, and the importance of a human approach to life.

Ubuntu is humanism, and the human being takes priority in all human conduct: "The value, dignity, safety, welfare, health, beauty, love and development of the human being, and respect for the human being are to come first, and should be promoted to first rank before all other considerations, particularly, in our time, before economic, financial, and political factors are taken into consideration. That is the essence of humanism, is the essence of Ubuntu / Botho" (Vilikazi, 1991:70).

Oduro (2006:1) describes Ubuntu as manifesting in group solidarity, mutual support, respect for human dignity, a de-emphasis on individualism, a culture of esprit de corps and the existence of a "we" – feeling.

The emphasis of these descriptions seems to be broadly based on the practical and spiritual experience of humanity or humanness. Humanness embraces the values of non-discrimination, cooperation, cohesion, goodness, dignity and someone striving to master the life-coping skill of being a person.

A Xhosa proverb that is of cardinal importance in the process of understanding Ubuntu, states:

"Ubuntu ungamuntu ngabanye abantu" – People are people through other people.

In the same sense a king is a king through his followers, and a manager is a manager through his colleagues/teammates.

Linguistically, Mfenyana (1986:2) alleges that in order to understand the full meaning of the word Ubuntu, the prefix "ubu" must first be separated from the root "-ntu". Ubu refers to the abstract. Ntu is an ancestor who spawned human society and gave them their way of life as human beings.

It is a communal way of life which deems that society must be managed for the good of all, thereby requiring cooperation as well as sharing and charity. For example, no widows or orphans should be left to fend for themselves - they all belong to someone. Consequently, Ubuntu is the quality of being human, and being human means being human through other human beings.

Ubuntu can therefore be defined as a comprehensive ancient African world view based on the values of intense humanness, caring, sharing, respect, compassion and associated values, ensuring a happy and qualitative communal way of life, in the spirit of family.

Ubuntu, being a world view, determines and influences everything a person thinks, says and does. And is it not interesting that what you think surfaces in the words you use, and is it not interesting that what you say also influences the way you act, walk, sit?

A world view determines the character of a person, and in turn the character of a person is indicative of the world view he or she subscribes to.

UBUNTU
IN OTHER AFRICAN LANGUAGES

The importance of sound human relations is found all over the continent of Africa. This affection with human beings is visible in the strong sense of togetherness and belonging. People generally refer to the continent as Mother Africa, i.e. as belonging to all the human beings living in Africa in the spirit of familyhood.

It is for this reason that words describing Ubuntu or humanness are found in all the African languages.

Here are a few examples (Broodryk, 2005:12).

isiZulu	**Ubuntu ***
seSotho	**Botho ***
Akan (Ghana)	**Biakoye**
Yoruba	**Ajobi**
Shangaan	**Numunhu**
shiVenda	**Vhuthu**

xiTsonga	**Bunhu**
isiXhosa (Transkei)	**Umntu**
Shona (Zimbabwe)	**Nunhu**
Kiswahili (Tanzania)	**Ujamaa**
Swahili (Kenya)	**Utu**
Ugandan	**Abantu**
English	**Humanness**
Cape Afrikaans	**Menslikgeit**
Afrikaans	**Mensheid/medemenslikheid**

* (A combination of these words is often used to cover both these languages, in the term "Ubuntu-Botho". The meaning, however, remains the same).

(In Belgium a book - the exact particulars of which are not known to the author - was published in the Flemish language on the experience of a coloured male who lived in the Western Cape, where Ubuntu was referred to as "oeboentoe". The word "oeboentoe" also appears to be the correct version in phonetic Afrikaans.)

The PROMINENCE OF UBUNTU

In an article (Du Preez, 2006:14) under the heading "Ubuntu is hijacked, we must save it" a plea is made that a first big project by the intellectual gents of the Native Club (an elite forum influenced by the President of South Africa) should be to establish a means of ensuring that Ubuntu is protected and not misused by sinister individuals or power groups to obtain their own selfish goals, since "most South Africans agree that Ubuntu is a uniquely African way of approaching life".

This prominence of Ubuntu is reflected as being both a constitutional and non-constitutional base in South African life.

Constitutionally, it forms the national value base of the official Constitution of the Republic of South Africa (especially the section on Human Rights), it is part of the vision and mission of the transformation of the new public service (the so-called Batho Pele principles), it is a principle upon which all future welfare policies will be based, and part of the White Paper of various government departments like the Departments of Social Development and of Education.

Ubuntu is being taught in various schools as part of the subject Guidance and its values are captured in the framework of national education, as part of the curricula of various courses at tertiary institutions.

These include courses in education, educational philosophy, philosophy, business economics, law, anthropology, sociology, welfare, development administration, political science, psychology and religion.

It is also the value base of several non-government organisations and the business philosophy of various companies in the private sector, like banks, life insurance companies, retail stores, electricity suppliers, airlines and television stations.

A series of television programmes with the title Heartlines were broadcast by the three SABC television channels from July-September 2006 to highlight what happened if people do not practise the typical national values of compassion, forgiveness, responsibility, honesty, self-control, caring, love, and perseverance. These well-propagated series were an attempt to remind citizens of the importance of honouring the afore mentioned values and they were all illustrated with real-life situations to showcase the practical implementation of Ubuntu. The Ubuntu icon, former President Nelson Mandela, gave a foreword message to the nation to strengthen the relevant messages of the series.

First National Bank (FNB) donated millions of "values wristbands" to members of the public who supported these positive values, as part of a constructive nation-building endeavour. The message in this campaign was that if everyone believes in the value of values, not just the value of money, the nation will benefit and become a rich nation. If everyone actively lives a value-based life, all will experience true wealth creation.

At the 9th Educational Management Association International Conference on Ubuntu (2006) at Bela-Bela, Limpopo Province, it was proposed that the possibility be investigated of making the teaching of Ubuntu part of the formal school system in all the countries of Africa.

The reasoning was that Ubuntu has been part and parcel of life in Africa, throughout centuries, and that young people need to be educated about the traditional values of Africa. This will assist in the regeneration of the traditional Ubuntu values, and their consequent manifestation in life-coping skills, where they have been lost or forgotten.

The basic-life coping skills of Ubuntu, as will be indicated in later chapters in this book, are also applicable to other cultures and may even be taught on a global basis.

This practical possibility was also raised (Broodryk, 2006:2) at an international educational management conference in Cyprus, since many cultures have already been applying certain values and principles of Ubuntu.

UBUNTU VALUES

Values are closely related to norms or social rules - they are codes laid down by society, stipulating what constitutes acceptable behaviour. Values are about what should be done or how a person should behave.

Chinkanda (1990:1) describes Ubuntu as a term derived from "muntu", meaning a person, a human being. It defines a positive quality which a person supposedly possesses (an internal state of being or the very essence of being human). The values of Ubuntu manifest in good deeds like alms-giving, being sympathetic, being caring and sensitive to the needs and wants of others, being respectful, considerate, patient, kind and all other positive human qualities.

In Africa, values are the assegais (weapons, spears) you use to defend, manage and construct your own personal life and influence or protect that of a brotherhood. The assegai is alleged (Mandela, 1994:39) to symbolise all that is glorious and true in African history - it is a symbol of the African as a warrior and as an artist. What is glorious and true is reflected in the ancient historical values of Africa.

Values can also be seen as the basic foundations of each person's view of how life should be lived. They influence your choices, attitudes as well as your goals in life. Since they are accompanied by strong feelings, it is proposed that they be regarded as someone's assegais in both his or her cultural and general life.

Personal values are consequently to be revisited, especially in the context of the philosophy of Ubuntuism. Core values will be presented and their counterparts or associated values will also be identified since primary values can usually be linked to other secondary values.

Values are values because of other values.

They are derived from the Ubuntu world view, where the basic values of humanness, caring, sharing, respect and compassion are of cardinal importance for practical "living" and enjoying a life which is cemented in true, genuine and selfless happiness.

The core values of Ubuntu are (Broodryk, 2005:174) humanness, caring, sharing, respect and compassion.

These core values are associated with various other positive values, like

➢ warmth, tolerance, understanding, peace, humanity (related to humanness)

➢ empathy, sympathy, helpfulness, charity, friendliness (related to caring)

➢ giving (unconditional), redistribution, open-handedness (related to sharing)

➢ commitment, dignity, obedience, order, the normative (related to sharing)

➢ love, cohesion, informality, forgiveness, spontaneity (related to compassion).

These core and associated values will be discussed separately in the following chapters.

Living according to certain values provides some sort of satisfaction or happiness. All other cultures may also claim to "live" the liberal ideal of happiness. This happiness, however, excludes certain African customs like natural warmth and spontaneity: Affectionate Africans experience some European cultures as being cold and exclusive.

The Ubuntu way of "living" happiness may be portrayed as being more intense and genuine, and is closely interwoven with other precious core and associated ancient values.

CASE STUDY:
CAPTIVES OF TAXI VIOLENCE

Taxis in a certain part of Soweto, which is a popular tourist destination in South Africa, have become involved in a war in which envious and competitive taxi owners make use of violent means to eliminate the competition.

In a serious shooting incident police have been called out to rescue passengers travelling in two taxis. Fortunately, only four passengers are now caught in the cross-fire, but unfortunately they find themselves in different areas of the taxi rank.

The situation is extremely dangerous and their lives are in danger.

The issue is: Who should be rescued first in terms of the aforementioned primary values?

You have only ten minutes to come to a decision. (This can be done in a group discussion or in smaller groups.)

The four trapped people are:

Derek A. Coutts: Derek is 46 years old, a computer consultant from New Zealand who is working temporarily in South Africa.

This is his last month in the country and he merely wished to visit the Hector Pietersen memorial and museum so that he can inform his friends abroad of the struggle that took place in Soweto.

As a humanitarian his intention is also to raise money in New Zealand for those infected with HIV/AIDS. He hopes to raise R4 million for this cause in the next three months.

Jimmy Ntuku: Jimmy is a youth leader and is highly respected in Soweto for his community development work. He has recently paid lobola, since he is going to marry a rural woman from KwaZulu-Natal within the next month. He has a bright future ahead of him.

Hermina Dibetso: Hermina is an old woman who has been suffering from an as yet undiagnosed illness. She needs to visit a clinic urgently because her blood pressure is very high. If she does not receive treatment she fears that serious complications may set in.

Frans Nel: Frans is a white Afrikaner who became an anti-apartheid activist during the struggle years. The purpose of his visit is to investigate the possibility of making a film about Soweto and its people, to show the world how the inhabitants of the township live Ubuntu every day. If he is successful, he will make millions of Rand for himself. He might, however, donate half of his profits to charity.

Discuss and report back.

The Value of Humanness 3

"Ubuntu is the art of being a human person."
— *Mfuniselwa John Bhengu* (1996:13)

INTRODUCTION

The basic point of departure in conceptualising the phenomenon of Ubuntu, is to understand the comprehensive applicability of humanness, which is different from humanity or humanism.

Humanness respects all religions and world views. Humanism, in its modern context, is a reference to the thinking that all religious beliefs should be rejected and that the only issue which should be at stake is the promotion of human welfare.

Humanness is a permanent ingredient of a certain lifestyle, whilst any deed of kindness to another person is a once-off or temporary manifestation of humanity.

Humanness is intense and practised sincerely, while humanity is general and practised as a sign of goodwill. Humanness, with the emphasis on "-ness" as a spiritual manifestation of a human-centered person(s), appears to be the best word in the English language with which to describe Ubuntu to others.

An example of humanness is observed when an empathic person identifies him or herself with the problems and suffering of others in an understanding way. He or she treats all human beings equally. The human person shows his or her humanity visibly in the way he or she treats both persons and the environment.

Humanness is the main component of Ubuntu. In this sense Ubuntu humanness is compared (Ramose, 1998: 49) with the African tree of knowledge. The surrounding soil, root, stem, branches and leaves as a unit make up the perception of a tree. Similarly, the core values and associated values of Ubuntu form the perception of the tree of humanness. This conception of Ubuntu is comprehensive and includes the rights of a human being.

All human beings benefit from their basic human rights which need to be respected, and it is claimed (Ibid::81), that all theories of human rights involve the facet of being human – the humanness aspect that is Ubuntu – as their point of departure. These human rights theories attribute value to or determine the worth of the very facet of being human. The primary focus of human rights is on human relations.

A living human being deserves recognition by all other human beings. In this sense, theories on human rights are ultimately concerned with one fundamental, basic human right – the right to life.

The right to life concerns the freedom or liberty of the individual to strive constantly to defend and protect life. Purposive human activity is hence first and foremost oriented towards the preservation of individual life.

The right to life implies the human rights to freedom of speech and thought, freedom of association, the right to work, and to own property.

Human rights to life tolerate different applications of the values and norms of different cultures. Generally gratefulness is a value which is common to most cultures, but it may be applied differently by all of them. As noted it is, for instance, customary in Africa for the husband-to-be to reward his future parents-in-law with cattle (or in modern times with money) as a show of appreciation for the woman they raised, while this is an unknown custom in other cultures. Other cultures have, however, no right to be prejudiced about this show of gratitude.

Citizens have the right to voice their personal beliefs regarding life, politics and religion. Opposing viewpoints should therefore be tolerated in the spirit of humanness and democracy.

The right to work and to be empowered for work are fundamental human rights. People should be encouraged to build their capacity and receive training to be able to perform effectively in a work situation.

Africans have always attached value to the subsistence farming enterprise system, which is also a way of living in harmonious co-existence with families and extended families. The freedom to own property for such purposes is therefore a logical right.

The tradition, however, was that land belonged to all. The community – and not an individual was therefore the landlord.

The right to life also affects many facets in the life of a person.

It is a taboo for a responsible person living with a sexual disease like HIV/AIDS to spread this disease to his loved one(s) and other persons, because the disease is killing people.

Taboos were learnt by means of oral education.

Oral education in the form of dramatised storytelling took place in the absence of written material. African people make extensive use of body language in their daily communications – especially when reporting a specific incident or when involved in storytelling. Storytelling is so dramatised that it has developed into what is branded "narrative therapy", meaning that the attention of the audience is captured to such an extent that their minds cannot wander entertain other ideas or thoughts. This is called narrative flow. Flow in general indicates that a person's mind is 100% engrossed in a certain activity, for example when climbing dangerous rocks, or playing a complex chess game.

More often than not, the practise of narrative therapy involves sounds related to animal noises, to bring about or heighten a flow situation. Animals are highly respected and are believed to communicate with humans. Animals are seen as friends, and hunting them for the mere pleasure of doing so (and not for the purpose of eating), is an unknown and unacceptable practice in Africa.

Humanness, the inherent Ubuntu quality, will therefore also determine how a human being treats animals and even surrounding physical environment he finds himself in.

Human Rights

Humanness is formally protected by the highest legal authority. The Constitution of the Republic of South Africa has been hailed by the Secretary-General of the United Nations (UN), Kofi Annan, as beacon of tolerance, peaceful co-existence and mutual respect (Beeld, 16 March 2006:14).

According to Annan, South Africa serves as an example to the world for the way in which it deals with heated feelings of wrath based on historical incidents, and with misunderstandings flowing from differences in culture and religious beliefs.

The Constitution is characterised by its Ubuntu influences. In the final moments of the development of the Constitution Ubuntu was actually verbalised in the document, but the word "ubuntu" was replaced by references to concepts related to human rights.

The Ubuntu values, however, have remained in the formal Bill of Rights.

In the second chapter of the Constitution, under the heading Bill of Rights, Ubuntu themes like the following are highlighted:

➢ equality
➢ human dignity
➢ freedom of the person
➢ freedom of expression
➢ freedom of association
➢ freedom of trade, occupation, and profession
➢ tolerance towards cultural and religious beliefs
➢ the right to food and water
➢ the rights of children
➢ political rights
➢ the right to education.

Human dignity is appreciated in that everyone is seen as having inherent dignity, as well as the right to have their dignity respected and protected.

In South Africa 21 March is Human Rights Day – a day on which human rights are celebrated annually.

TOLERANCE

Meaningful co-existence implies that people should be very tolerant of one another.

Tolerance means to being accepting of all other opinions, cultures, faiths, ideological or political beliefs, and world views.

If people meet and have different opinions on specific issues, everyone who wants to speak should be free to do so. Even contradictory opinions should be respected.

In traditional Africa everyone was heard (Mandela, op cit: 20): Chief and subject, warrior and medicine man, shopkeeper and farmer, land-owner and labourer. People used to speak without being interrupted, and meetings lasted for hours – especially if a solution had to be found and people had different opinions on a matter. Eventually consensus – or some form of consensus – was reached: The majority did not crush the minority. This was African democracy in its truest form, and a brilliant example of tolerance in practice.

Children should acquire the skill of tolerance from a very young age. They have to be taught that there are many different cultures, beliefs, social customs/etiquettes and conventions in life, and there is a chance that these may be in direct conflict with what they have been brought up to believe. Some children are brought up to believe that only one specific religion is correct, and that this specific religion must be honoured exclusively, in a dogmatic way – the rest are doomed to hell or are perceived as a threat. From an Ubuntu perspective, this type of reasoning is wrong and not indicative of tolerance.

In traditional Africa, tolerance was interpreted in the broadest sense of the word – as concept which encompassed the freedom to practise different religions, which were all equally respected.

This form of tolerance included being lenient towards latecomers at indabas (conferences), so-called "tolerance time" or "African time". Tolerance time refers to the tendency towards non-punctuality, which is a controversial issue: Some Africans insist that "African time" does not exist, since time is time. In other words, why discriminate against Africans when non-punctuality appears in all cultures to a greater or lesser degree?

Others argue that the Western wristwatch shows European time, and that in the olden days in Africa watches did not exist. Traditionally time was measured by events like bedtime, mealtimes, and in particular sunrise and sunset – people rise at sunrise and bed down at sunset.

In its modern usage African time is a reference to people being late for meetings or work. This may be seen as not being peculiar to Africa alone, since people of all cultures sometimes arrive late for events. Their lateness could be due to the fact that they reside long distances away from work, or experience serious transport or other problems (taxi wars, strikes, unreliable modes of transport, ill health, family issues, death in the family, etc.).

Europeans are extremely time conscious and punctual: Their lives are dominated by watches. Punctuality is the norm which influences various actions. They adhere to the saying: Time is money.

These extreme time-conscious attitudes lead to serious stress-related problems, and you only have to look at all the worried faces of motorists during peak hour – people who fear they'll be late for work or an appointment – to understand how much Europeans value punctuality and how strictly they adhere to time constraints. No wonder stress in its many hidden forms is killing so many Europeans.

On the other hand, an African labourer may reason that the work never ends, and therefore he may regard rigid punctuality as not being all that important.

If the labourer is an illiterate who cannot even read time on a watch, how can anyone expect him to be punctual at all times?

In this respect you can argue that if the labourer is half an hour late, he may be allowed to work half an hour later. Call it flexi-time (productivity will remain the same)!

Other job categories will have to be treated differently, though. You expect pilots to be punctual because the nature of their work is different in respect of rigid time consciousness: If a pilot arrives at the airport whenever he wants to, it will cause complete and utter chaos.

UNDERSTANDING

People's opinions are often rejected due to misunderstandings.

Understanding emphasises the important skills of listening and practising empathy. Understanding is of cardinal importance as a life-coping skill. Understanding others helps you communicate better and make better decisions in everyday life situations. The words, and even the body language a person uses, are cardinal to understanding that person better. Words and vocabulary, as well as the way in which they are used (loud, soft, with arm movements to emphasise something, gestures, widening of the eyes, etc) are reflections, and in some cases even betrayers of what is happening in the mind!

Meaning must therefore be attached to the words a person uses and must indicate clearly the message being transferred. The intention (to trick, inform, report, etc), and context (to provoke laughter, provide relevant information or give feedback) of the message should be determined through attentive listening and observation.

Observation helps you notice messages of non-verbal communication. Body language, for example, manifests in physical movements, gestures and attitudes. A relaxed body sends out a different message than a tense expression does.

Expressions of joy are easily distinguished from expressions of sorrow or depression.

Leaders and other decision makers should make a special effort to understand their followers and teammates/colleagues.

As Mandela (ibid:479) comments: "...to lead one's people, one must also truly know them."

Peace

All prominent religions propagate peace.

In Christianity the basic lesson for good life advocates peace, and in the Muslim faith the very word "muslim" means peace.

Religion generally propagates peace, for example, many religious people greet others with the words "peace be upon you".

In South Africa, peaceful protests are allowed as an expression of citizens' democratic rights. The democratic movements related to (or in alliance with the ANC (political) party) all followed a peaceful strategy of mass action, similar to Ghandi's non-violent protests in India.

In a personal sense, a person should strive to acquire the skill of being at peace with all. It is a fact of life that as you do unto others, they will do unto you. What you sow, you will reap. If you practise peace and diplomacy in dealing with others, others will also be diplomatic in return.

It is wise to avoid arguments and refrain from becoming angry when there are differences. The skill is to stay calm and in control of emotions like anger; to be at peace with all the events and stressors of life.

Humanity

Humanity is a worldwide phenomenon and a general life tendency. It is characterised by gestures of goodwill towards other human beings.

As a general skill humanity determines the way one associates with others.

Humanity prescribes that a person be gentle towards other human beings.

In this respect you can play the role of the shepherd, by not enforcing your will brutally upon others but by associating with them in a human and friendly way, and providing your opinions or giving directives in a subtle manner.

The shepherd-style of association is based (Mandela: ibid:21) on the skill of staying behind the flock of sheep like a shepherd, "letting the most nimble go on ahead, whereupon the others will follow, not realising that all along they are being directed from behind".

Case Study: Robben Island Experience

Mandela (ibid:417) recalls that when he and other political prisoners were serving out sentences on Robben Island, there was a specific warder with the nickname "Zithulele" – the quiet one.

It is customary in Africa to give specific names to foreigners, to describe some aspect of that person.

Zithulele was the tolerant, peaceful and soft-spoken warder in charge of the quarry. He was soft on the prisoners and stood a great distance from them as they did physical work, and appeared not to interfere with what they did (planning and executing their tasks) as long as it was done in an orderly and effective manner.

He never berated the prisoners when he found them leaning on their spades to rest, or when talking (a human thing to do). As a result of his human behaviour, the prisoners responded in kind.

One day he came to the prisoners and said: "Gentlemen (a human and decent way of addressing others, even though they were prisoners), the rains have washed away the lines on the roads; we need 20 kilos of lime today. Can you help?"

This was not part of their normal prison duties, but since the warder had approached the prisoners as human beings, they agreed to help.

For discussion

Discuss the merits of dealing with people in a spirit of humanness and humanity (kindness).

Provide concrete examples from your own life experiences.

The Value of Caring   4

INTRODUCTION

Caring is an important pillar in the Ubuntu world view.

Caring embraces a variety of approaches, like the way one talks to and behaves towards others.

It is true that all cultures have caring attitudes, but in the Ubuntu culture this caring is of a very intense nature.

Caring is said (Kathholi, 1997:1) to be about loving, listening and accepting people.

Caring as life – coping skill reflects in the ability to treat others in a compassionate way.

It is how parents and adults treat children, how children behave towards parents, how married spouses behave towards each other, how the aged are tended to, how the disabled are looked after, how the underprivileged are assisted, and to which extent a person controls his emotions under all circumstances.

Many people tend to become irritated or annoyed when approached by beggars for a small financial contribution. The Ubuntu guideline in this respect will be to give.

Just give whatever you can afford or have, even if it is not money but some other commodities like fruit or vegetables.

Caring is about putting the problems, interests and circumstances of all others, including those of beggars, at a high level in a loving, empathic and sympathetic spirit.

Caring, in contrasdt to these harmonious approaches, also manifests in strong, intolerant moral expressions and behaviour.

It is, for example, unacceptable in the Ubuntu environment to be patient with social misbehaviour and injustices.

Examples of violence, aggression, social misbehaviour and serious malpractices are observable in all societies of the world.

In only one edition of a Sunday newspaper (Sunday Times, 23 July 2006) the headlines of articles read inter alia:

➢ Twisted killers in a warped society
➢ US must end slavish loyalty
➢ Congo at the crossroads
➢ Ta Mok: Cruellest of the Khmer Rouge
➢ The parties involved in the conflict and what they want
➢ Foul cry as Ali bout called off
➢ Somali leader calls for holy war against Ethiopia
➢ I was not bribed, says top Nigerian politician
➢ Killing of civilians hits new high in Iraq
➢ Israel calls up reservists
➢ India train blasts: four held
➢ The destruction of Lebanon must stop now
➢ Conspiracy theory thickens
➢ Insults fly as Public Protector bosses battle
➢ Thugs attack visiting delegates
➢ Idols star's dirty secrets exposed.

If newspapers reflect the true nature and essence of society like some weird mirror, we are in deep trouble. The images in the mirror (or what one sees) indeed very scary and reflect a very sombre, depressing and sick picture of society.

These incidents are, however, in direct contrast to the caring prescription of Ubuntu.

It is evident that in these events Ubuntu is absent and that its caring value has to be reintroduced or revived. On the other hand, it is also true that Ubuntu reflects the ideal situation and that people are bound to transgress.

In this sense it may be argued that establishing a true and infallible Ubuntu society is not a practical possibility. This should, however, not be a stumbling block. Human beings should strive to live out the Ubuntu ideals – especially the notion of caring for others. Caring for others by implication means caring for yourself:

A person is a person through other people

Caring goes hand in hand with loving attitudes.

Someone who loves and appreciates human beings, animals and the environment will also portray a caring personality.

In African life caring also manifests in the respectful and humble way elders and superiors are greeted and addressed.

In Sesotho the word "Ntate" is used to address an old man or respected father figure.

CARING AND CHILDREN

It is convention in Africa to take communal care of children. The children are disciplined and educated on values like caring for others not by the natural parents only, but also by all uncles and aunts of the extended family. Elders play a prominent role in the education of values and life skills. The greater, extended family forms a close-knitt community which exists for the welfare of all who belong to it. In this small, closed societal structure caring manifests in the sharing of everything one has on a material level. Caring is part of cultural education.

The sage Oginga Odinga recalls (Oruka, 1992:37) that he received his cultural education at the feet of the village elders. It was practice in Luoland (Kenya) during those years for youths to be educated by the elders. The elders were versed in in all matters of culture and education which were to be imparted to the children and youth. Children who were obedient to older persons were treated with a special "liking". As a result, children could rely on the best caring attitudes from their elders.

The need to take great care in bringing up children, cannot be overemphasised. If children grow up in an environment of care-giving it is logical that they, in turn, will pass on the skill of caring to others as well.

Children should be taught that it is acceptable to show caring love to parents, family members, friends and others. Caring love is made visible when people hug or greet each other passionately: Seeing another person should be a happy event. The opposite, which has to be avoided, is the act of merely giving a cold grin and mumbling "hi" to someone.

It is recommended that educational authorities also promote and foster the practice of caring. Caring on the part of the educational authorities can manifest in the way children are treated and attended to by teachers. This is observable in body language and the way ordinary language is used (language can be abusive and insensitive and it could have a life-long effect on children if erroneous perceptions are established, or wrong messages are received).

People who work with children should also control their volume of speech, since talking too loudly may be mistaken for aggression or a loss of temper – both of which will be experienced negatively.

The process of teaching children positive life customs is much like playing the role of a gardener. While in prison, Mandela (ibid:478) began to order books on gardening and horticulture, but eventually learned through trial and error how to garden effectively. A garden was one of the few things in prison which one could control. Planting a seed, watching it grow, tending it and harvesting its fruit offered a simple, but enduring satisfaction.

In some ways, Mandela saw the garden as a metaphor for certain aspects of his life. A leader (or any person for that matter) must tend his garden, nurture it continuously, cultivate and harvest the fruit of his labours. All persons must take responsibility for what they cultivate.

EMPATHY

Empathy as a skill enables one to put oneself in another person's shoes. The ideal of empathy is contained in the ability to perceive the world or a specific situation precisely as the other person experiences it – in other words, the ability to enter into another's personality and imaginatively experience the fate of another.

Mastering this skill enables one to understand the experiences of others, which leads to a better understanding of and improved communication with others. Empathy thus enables a person to share in the joys and sorrow of others, as a way of caring.

Moreover, empathy provides perspective in your association with friends, those in need and loved ones.

In any form of negotiation, empathetic skills are essential. By placing oneself in the situation of the other party, a better picture of the motives or reasons for the argumentation of the other party is obtained. In this way greater clarity is obtained as to how positive resolutions can be reached and how a strategy communication can be developed.

Empathy is closely related to intensive listening and sympathy. Practising these skills correctly will result in genuine empathy as opposed to pretended empathy. Pretended empathy implies that the art of empathy has not been mastered, usually due to a lack of concentrated listening and genuine sympathy.

SYMPATHY

Sympathy is about the ability to successfully enter the emotional situation or feelings of others, which pertains to the manner in which one responds to the emotions of another person.

Humanness expects people to acquire the life skill of expressing sympathy to those in mourning, to those living in misery and even to the fate of offenders, since it is human to falter.

Human beings are not perfect, and history has numerous examples of good leaders making wrong or bad decisions.

Expressing sympathy has the benefit of enriching the sympathiser spiritually, because the person showing sympathy is actually reflecting something of his own inner divinity. If we all reflect a little bit of inner divineness, the sum total of this divine brotherhood will result in a peaceful and meaningful co-existence on Earth.

Sympathy is very much a brotherly or sisterly skill, meaning that the one who is suffering will receive the condolences of people who are almost like family. Condolences can also be expressed in a simple way, like just being present when someone needs company. Expressing your condolences or feelings of sympathy in words may not be necessary in some situations. Certain body language or gestures – like a hug or a pat on the shoulder – may be enough to show sympathy. These gestures indicate that you share in the problems facing someone else.

If happiness that is shared leads to more mutual happiness, the same notion applies to unhappiness: Shared unhappiness is easier to bear.

 HELPFULNESS

A person who is helpful will always be the salt of the earth.

Ubuntu demands that people help one another, especially in times of need or sorrow.

Regarding everyday life, Ndaba (1993:4) teaches that helpfulness can be illustrated in small acts like giving a pedestrian a lift without the motive of gaining financial compensation.

Helpfulness is further illustrated through acts like helping old people cross a street, standing so an elderly person can take your seat on a bus or train, and assisting ladies with heavy shopping bags.

CHARITY

There is a well-known saying: Charity begins at home. The person who gives unconditionally is acting in true Ubuntu spirit. Now the moral question arises of how one should treat beggars. People seem to be reluctant to give money to beggars since these donations may create dependency. If people are begging, the Ubuntu solution could be to donate one's surplus food or drink to beggars. Nobody should be suffering from hunger and thirst.

As the saying goes: There but for the grace of God, go you and I. Ubuntu will probably reason that it is divine to give – therefore, just give.

FRIENDLINESS

Ubuntu people are the friendliest people imaginable. In Africa, it is tradition to be extremely friendly and hospitable.

Africans embody true hospitality. This has been noted since the first time Europeans started recording their experiences with Africans in written format.

Moodie (1960:431) refers to an incident in 1686 when the Dutch ship Stavenisse was shipwrecked off the KwaZulu-Natal coast. The survivors spent three years living among the Xhosa and could not believe the friendliness or caring attitudes of the Africans: "In their intercourse they were polite, civil, extremely talkative, saluting each other, whether male or female, whenever they meet, asking whence they come, and whither they are going, what is their news...one may travel two hundred or three hundred mylen through the country without any fear from men. Neither need one be in any apprehension about meat and drink, as they have in every village or kraal a house of entertainment for travellers, where these are not only lodged, but fed also."

In Kenya the cheerful locals use the word "Jambo" (meaning "Hello") whenever they come into contact with foreigners or tourists. They do not have a hidden agenda when being friendly, since greetings are exchanged in a natural way. On the contrary, greeting in a friendly manner shows respect for other people: It shows that visitors are recognised as human beings in simple "Utu" (the Swahili word for Ubuntu) terms. These are the kinds of people who smile as they share whatever they have with strangers.

Traditional dances are accompanied by a happy beating of the drums, and even the taxis play friendly tunes on their hooters as they canvass passengers from the streets.

Africans are spontaneous folk who laugh easily in a natural, loud and joyous way (from deep down in the pit of the stomach). Africans generally believe that Westerners, on the other hand, cannot laugh – they can only grin!

CASE STUDY: THE ECHO OF LIFE

A sage (African wise man) invited his youngest son to climb the highest peak of a mountain with him. Apart from it being a strenuous exercise, his intention was to teach his son the very basic tenets of good life, and about the meaning or sense of life.

They climbed the steep mountain in short distances at a time, in the way lions eat an elephant: Piece by piece.

Once they reached the top of the mountain the son, overwhelmed by the beauty of the scenery and the golden silence, exclaimed:

"Baba (Dad), this view is fantastic!"

Immediately his voice and the words he had uttered were returned in the same volume, or maybe even louder, by the mountain itself (or so the son thought).

"Baba, this view is fantastic!"

Excited and amazed, the son shouted these words again and again, and they seemed to return to him twice as loud each time.

Eventually the boy asked his wise father to explain what was happening.
His father told him that what he was hearing was an echo.

"Whatever you scream, shout or say out loud, the mountain will echo back in its voice precisely what you say, only twice as loud."

"But," he said, "this is also a lesson of life. Whatever you do to fellow human beings, your deeds will one day come back to you in duplicate – just like this echo. It may be almost identical to this experience, but know for sure that it will come back to you in some way. Therefore be very careful of how you treat human beings, life and the ones you love, because in turn they will always treat you in the very same way."

"Always be nice, friendly, caring, peaceful, respectful and compassionate, and in return you can be assured of a harmonious and joyous walk throughout the wonderful mountains and valleys of life."

Mountains are exciting because they exist as obstacles that must be conquered. The world consists of valleys as well, and if you cannot conquer a mountain you should leave it, because you must leave what you cannot conquer. Rather enjoy the valleys then. Life is too short and precious for a human being to waste time trying to conquer the unconquerable.

In Africa, the ultimate life test of successful parenthood is whether children offer – of their own accord – to look after their parents. It is common practice for parents to provide only the best care for their children, knowing that those children will in turn care for and look after them when they are old.

For discussion

Exercise 1: A brainstorming exercise: Do you agree with this lesson?

➢ Do you know people who enjoy life due to their pleasant and caring personalities? Elaborate.

➢ Would you also like to be like such a person?

➢ Do you know how to go about becoming such a person?

➢ Write down five steps which you think you should take, in order to reach this goal.

Ponder on these steps.

Repeat this exercise after reading this book, and then compare your answers: Do findings differ?

Exercise 2: Draw a sketch to illustrate how you experience yourself at this moment in time. For example: Look in the mirror and draw what your face portrays – the state of your hair (if you have any); your eyes (are they healthy and friendly, or swollen, puffy and red like the morning after the night before); your nose and mouth. More important, though, is the expression on your face.

Is there a smile or a frown? Does your face show worry or ignorance? A mirror never lies: What you see in the mirror is a reflection of your true self.

Repeat this exercise after reading this book. In other words, make another sketch of yourself after you have completed the final chapter.

Ponder on the results.

Let's name them *Before* and *After* sketches:

Do you notice any differences in your appearance in the two sketches?

Are the expressions identical or different?

Are there any **specific reasons** why your expression in the *After* sketch is different from that of the *Before* sketch ?

The Value of Sharing 5

"If you have two cows, and the milk of the first cow is enough for your own consumption, Ubuntu expects you to donate the milk of the second cow to your underprivileged brother and sister"

― *Walter Sisulu* (1993:1)

INTRODUCTION

To share is to give, to donate, to have something in common, or to distribute.

Sharing is a simple but often-neglected life skill, but not all people are prepared to share their possessions, assets and even their knowledge with others. Alternatively, one finds that some have hidden agendas when they do in fact share.

In the Ubuntu culture it is normal cultural practice to share willingly. "Mahala" is a conventional and traditional African concept that says it is fine to give something free of charge to others, and not to expect anything in return.

Traditionally the sharing way of life was illustrated (Oruka, 1992, op cit:37) through the issues of land and cattle. The individuals of the community shared land. The land belonged to the community and not to an individual. No one person or group could be allowed to sell any part of land to outsiders or acquire it for exclusive personal or family use. Every individual family had a piece or several pieces of land designated as theirs. This concept of "theirs" did not mean exclusively theirs. It was provisionally theirs. Any member of the community had a right to a piece from those who had. A community as a whole could acquire any piece of land for collective use.

In each community all the cattle used common fields for grazing. It was not possible for an individual to sell an inch of those fields as his possession: Fields were communal.

Individuals without cattle had the privilege of borrowing from those who had. The products would then be shared fairly between the two parties. The original owner received, for example, two out of three calves produced, leaving one to the borrower. The borrower would, in addition, be entitled to all the milk.

Although the communities were poor in regard to material luxuries, starvation was eliminated by the willingness of the members of that community to share with those who were suffering.

No family would be allowed to starve while an other was in a position to feed itself. In the same way those who had would just give whatever food and drink they had.

The culture of giving is highlighted by means of certain comrade-related activities like the sharing of all physical objects.

A comrade-type activity is, for instance, praying a visit to a hospital – not only to see a sick relative or friend, but also even to visit those patients whom you do not know. This is also not meant to be a clinical and speedy visit: Patients should be approached in a warm manner, and in-depth inquiries should be made about their circumstances, or possible assistance which can be rendered to them. Examples are notifying relatives when someone has been admitted to hospital, sending letters to others, helping to pay the patient's most urgent bills (like water and lights) or handling anything that requires immediate attention.

Regarding the sharing of food, it is still the convention in African culture to donate and it is regarded as an insult to others if an individual does not share food. This convention also applies to refreshments not being shared by all at meetings, events, or in the workplace. Africans grow up sharing food with other family members and neighbours. When people visit a family they may find they are given preference and allowed to eat first.

One ethical issue which deserves greater attention is the extent to which you are morally obliged to share your belongings with others.

Is it, for instance, moral to drive a luxury car in an environment where nobody possesses a car?

...to live in luxury in an environment where others have no shelter?

...to eat in exclusive restaurants when others have to scavenge on dumping sites for food that is often rotten and hazardous to their health?

These are real, practical dilemmas.

The answer probably lies within each person's conscience. If your conscience does not haunt you for living in abundance without sharing, there is not much that can be done to change the situation: You cannot compel people by law to be morally conscious. It is a matter of heart. Heartless people will ignore the ethical expectations of Ubuntu.

Within an Ubuntu environment it is normal to feed those with no income, in a spirit of sharing. This is also a convention aimed at reducing the effects of poverty, namely for those with an income to provide for those without an income. A shebeen (pub, bar, drinking place) is a respected and dignified but very informal venue for uninhibited socialisation. In one observation it was noted that several individuals were seated around a table as a group. The first person stood up and bought drinks for the whole group. Once the drinks were finished, the second person stood up and ordered another round for everyone.

After finishing those, the third person remained seated without offering to buy a round. Eventually the fourth person, without any protest, stood up and bought another round for everybody. This was accepted in the greatest harmony, in spite of the third person not buying any drinks. The reason for this apparently odd behaviour is simple: The third person did not have the material means (money) to buy a round. This, however, did not exclude him from enjoying several drinks which were paid for by the other members of the group. In this example the group members realised he had no money, or they may have known that he had to use what he had for something more important, like providing food for his family. They also instinctively accepted that once their friend was in a better position (financially speaking), he would contribute to the socialising process again.

Another form of sharing is to contribute to the well-being or solving of a dilemma a person finds himself in. In this respect Sisulu (ibid:1) refers to the example of the assistance people rendered when it was time to plough the fields. Those with cattle would loan their oxen to those without cattle so they could plough the land. The cattle owners never expected anything in return. The cattle were provided without question – something which was accepted with gratitude.

Sharing and family

People should be helped to acquire the virtue of sharing at a very young age, and apart from educational institutions the family should influence children in especially the early stages of childhood, to develop giving and sharing mentalities. Children should be taught that it is through giving that they will also receive when it matters.

In the school milieu children should feel free to share all that they have in an unselfish way, and to suppress feelings or ideas of greed: Individual greed and selfishness are two of the major stumbling blocks impeding harmonious interpersonal human relations.

Schools should, in the true spirit of Ubuntu, consider introducing a money kitty system to enable those children who have, to donate their extra pocket money to those who do not have. Those who do not have should receive money from this kitty without having to feel shy or inhibited in accepting it: It is a fact of life that some will have, while others will not. Children should live out this truth, and heed the recommendation that those who have, share. Learning to do this from an early age will engender a culture of natural sharing.

GIVING UNCONDITIONALLY

Few people are prepared to give what they have unconditionally.

The Western way of life tends to make individuals more selfish and individualistic than their African counterparts. In the African milieu people tend to share, and wealthier people regard it as an honour to give to those in need.

The ideal of basic living and unconditional giving seems relatively easy. How much food does one person really need to consume?

If one has too much, it is advisable to give to others without laying down conditions: This is also a form of redistribution.

REDISTRIBUTION AND GREED

It is recommended that you redistribute your excess resources to the needy.

Mandela (op cit:307) recalls an embarrassing situation while imprisoned on Robben Island. Thanks to the generosity of his visitors he received a lot of fruit which he wanted to share with his fellow prisoners. This was strictly forbidden. He subsequently offered some of the food to the warders. Only after one of the warders had decided to eat one of the apples, was Mandela allowed to redistribute the surplus food to his fellow prisoners!

Redistribution can also apply to non-physical needs like knowledge. The learned have a moral responsibility to share their knowledge with those who are not learned, especially with the illiterates.

OPEN-HANDEDNESS

An open hand indicates that a person is prepared to donate to those in need.

A closed hand may be symbolic of selfishness, which goes against the grain of Ubuntu.

In Kenya an Akamba proverb warns that a person who eats alone, dies alone (Mbiti in Mwakabana, 2002:83). This proverb is used to highlight the value of sharing both joy (food) and sorrow (death). If there is no fellowship, i.e. no sharing of food during your life, there will be no sharing of grief and bereavement at your funeral.

According to Ndaba (in Broodryk, 1995:4) the greatest insult an African can give another person is to declare that he or she will not attend their funeral. The reason for this is that death is a very serious event in African life, since this is the period in which the spirit of a man leaves the physical body to become part of the ever-present world of the ancestors.

ᴄASE STUDY:
THE GREEDY POULTRY FARMER

A very rich but greedy poultry farmer, who refused to redistribute part of his wealth to others in need, employed hundreds of labourers on his farm. He was known to be autocratic and apart from being extremely selfish, he underpaid his labourers. One evening, the child of one of the labourers became sick. The child was crying for food so the mother begged the worker to "take" and slaughter one of the farmer's chickens which she wanted to cook for the child.

The labourer eventually stole one of the chickens and gave it to his spouse to cook for the sick child.

When the farmer discovered the theft he called in the police, who arrested the labourer. The labourer was sentenced to three months imprisonment for theft, and also lost his job.

For discussion

Examine the moral issue in terms of Ubuntu:

Was this indeed theft?
Should the police have arrested the labourer, or not?
Should he perhaps have taken eggs instead?
Is the farmer someone of immense greed?
What is the lesson of this case study?

The Value of Respect   6

"Can there be anything more important than looking after one🏻s ageing mother?"

— *Nelson Mandela* (op cit:19)

INTRODUCTION

Generally, respect indicates obedience (legal aspects, rules, conventions), honour (values and traditions), and consideration (the fate of others, taking account of, to refrain from discrimination and selfish actions).

Respect is an important concept in the Ubuntu lifestyle, and it is related to discipline, law and order. Known as "ukuhlonipha" in isiZulu, it is regarded (Mdluli, 1987:67) as the most central theme of the Ubuntu world view.

Ubuntu embraces a number of customary rules that govern relationships at different levels of society. Respect stipulates the authority elders have over young people, parents over children, leaders over followers, and (traditionally) men over women. It not only emphasises respect for the people one knows, but also for those one does not know.

In African society, man is the most important element and each person is dependent on the goodwill and acceptance of others.

One therefore has to conform to the values of Ubuntu, which include showing respect to all and in return getting respect from all.

Respect is shown to all members of the community, irrespective of their academic and material status. Literates and illiterates are treated equally. A labourer is also a highly respected person and is not inferior to a professional person. Children are highly honoured but in turn they are expected to show respect for cultural resources.

Cultural resources refer to the lessons a community has learned and carried forward from the past. These resources indicate how human beings have developed and how the community has evolved. Resources include folk songs, ancient stories, traditional rituals, artwork, architecture and life-coping lessons. Included are the beliefs and faiths of what previous generations upheld, did, said, thought and created. These resources form the laws, morals, ethics and principles that the community have been developed throughout the ages.

Traditionally, four conventions regarding the value of respect were honoured:

➢ Youths had to respect elders and do as they were told without questioning

➢ The man was the head of the family and the woman played a different role, namely as care-giver (Westerners and other cultures may regard the role of traditional women as inferior, but this not the intention).

➢ Respect had (at all times) to be shown to authority, irrespective of whether or not one agreed with the view of the authority figure. In order for things to run smoothly in all kinds of work situations, there were people to manage such undertakings. If you were at work, no matter what job you did (even mine labourers), it was important to respect superiors at all times

➢ The law had to be strictly adhered to.

Respect is shown in humility.

A humble person is generally regarded as respecting others. This manifests in the way superiors are approached, the unconditional sharing of food and drink with other / underprivileged persons or strangers, and even with the ancestors. Ancestors are highly respected and not forgotten during everyday life, festivals or celebrations.

Respect manifests in behaviour, like the way in which you obey leaders and authority figures, welcome strangers, and also how you deal with others.

The Ubuntu norms and values of the community are similarly respected since they determine life in that community. If a community member has offended someone, other extended family members collectively become involved in discussing the offence in order to settle the problem and restore peace and unity.

Respect is especially applicable to the manner in which elders are treated. Elders are regarded as wise people due to the life skills and knowledge they have acquired over the years.

Traditionally, communities looked after their aged – something which nullified the need for old-age homes. An old-age home is an unknown phenomenon in traditional Africa. The aged are highly respected for what they have done for their children, and for the wisdom they share with youngsters. It is a form of an annuity or pension where children guarantee that their elders can retire inclusively within their extended family, and not exclusively in an old-age home outside of the family.

To command respect, job status is not as important as a person's age. A younger person who occupies a senior position is expected to honour older people, in spite of them perhaps occupying more inferior work positions. A young managing director will therefore treat an elderly gardener or tea lady with as much respect as he would any other senior staff member.

In Kenya the so-called sages are regarded as wise people and philosophical counsellors. They are approached for solutions to everyday problems.

In rural KwaZulu-Natal, in South Africa, it is found (Broodryk, 1995:10) that old women in the villages or kraals are generally regarded as wise. The chief (or leader) of the village assigns a special hut to the oldest woman, from where she teaches children about Ubuntu tradition and values. She also advises adults on solving everyday problems.

The oral way of teaching and storytelling is an important tradition in African life and it is customary to tell moral tales around the magic of the African fire. Members of the community, especially youngsters, assemble around the fire at night with an elder telling moral stories or teaching life lessons. This is done in quite a dramatic way, therefore storytelling has developed into a respected African artform.

Africa is said (Savory, op cit:Introduction) to have a wonderfully rich store of folktales that have been passed down from one generation to the next. There are stories about how the world came into being, tales that tell of the relationships between human beings, and between man and his environment, as well as the lessons to be learned from everyday experiences. The tales are like the fairytales told all over the world, but they have a strong African flavour that is as real as the smell of rain on the warm earth.

These tales take the listener into an enchanted world where animals can talk, where human beings change into different life forms and magic is commonplace. Despite numerous setbacks, things usually turn out all right in the end – which is very much in line with positive thinking.

One example of such an African tale is called (ibid:93) "The Punishment of the Faithless One". It is a Matabele story which explains why the male Trumpeter Hornbill seals the entrance to the nest after the female has laid her eggs. He only leaves a small slit through which he can pass her food. The female is imprisoned inside until the young birds are old enough to be fed from outside by both parents. The reason for the female's imprisonment is due to the fact that she was once unfaithful to her husband and flirted with another handsome young male, leaving the eggs all on their own.

The objective of the story is to teach faithfulness between couples and spouses, which will ensure a happy and positive life together.

Faithfulness is a sign of respect for the other spouse, and it manifests in practical commitment.

COMMITMENT

Commitment as a skill implies a form of orderly planning, complete devotion and continuous self-motivation.
A committed person is easily recognisable in a group of people: He or she is the one who listens attentively, enquires in a sensible way and acts in an energised manner.
It is the person who persists with a task until it is fully completed.

In South Africa, it is common practice to call a close friend a "comrade". This practice is not related to any ideology: It is merely a way of addressing a committed friend or bosom buddy.

DIGNITY

A dignified person is someone with self-respect. The Ubuntu-oriented person will always strive to behave with dignity.

In this regard Ubuntu is described (Teffo, in Mkwakabana, op cit:38) as the human quality which reflects – and at the same time underpins – the dignity of a human personality. It is a cohesive moral value inherent to all humans.

Self-respect usually manifests in a person's behaviour towards others (it is tolerant, harmonious), in his or her choice of words and body language. People tend to favour dignified persons in positions of leadership and authority, since dignified persons portray some form of trustworthiness which they carry like an aura around them.

OBEDIENCE

The skill of obedience is evident in a person who abides by institutional and social restrictions. Laws, regulations and conventions are meant to instil order in any society.

Instilling a spirit of obedience is something that starts in childhood. Children are encouraged to respect authority, and to obey the requests or instructions of their elders.

It is true that elders – like people in general – should earn respect, which mean elders and parents should always behave in a dignified and loving manner towards children. This is how respect is acquired. Children will also be respected if they earn such respect by embodying positive attitudes and activities. It is a two-way process.

Ubuntu honours respect as a cardinal skill, since respect is the basis of a structured and disciplined society. If families are to be evaluated the question is not about anything else they should be judged on, but the respectful conventions that manifest and are upheld in that family: Being shown respect (or not) is an indication of whether a person is decent and civilised (or not).

Order

Respect is closely linked to the skill of living an ordered and structured life. Ubuntu societies were traditionally based on extended family systems.

In this respect Xhosa society is described (Mandela, op cit:4) as a proud and ordered unit with an expressive and euphonious language, and an abiding belief in the importance of laws (family), education and courtesy.

Xhosa society is a balanced and harmonious social order in which every individual knows his or her place.

Each Xhosa belongs to a clan that could trace its descent back to a specific forefather. Mandela, for example, is a member of the Madiba clan, named after a Themba chief who ruled in the Transkei during the 18th century. Mandela is often addressed as "Madiba", his clan name, as a sign of respect.

Family is generally regarded as the primary institution of any society. Some of the major functions of the family include socialisation, informal education (especially on norms and mores), and the transmission of values to young members of that society.

Order also refers to self-order. An example of this would be where an orderly person plans the execution of his activities in a prioritised way and deals with important issues first. A person who is well ordered usually plans his day from sunrise to sunset.

Carnegie (1936:78) describes this mode of planning as a life-coping skill, comparing life to living in different train compartments: Each day is a compartment on its own and the activities you should think and act upon, are primarily those related to the present-day compartments.

Tomorrow and yesterday are separate compartments and therefore secondary to the activities of today.

It boils down to the careful and effective budgeting of time.

There is a time for breakfast and other meals, a time to perform other activities like work, a time to meditate and celebrate, and a time to sleep.

Norms

In nature there are several examples of order which manifest in various norms or modes of behaviour. Flocks of birds migrate across the borders of countries and continents in an orderly manner, without causing traffic jams and smashing into each other. They follow their leader in a committed way to a specific destination – there is purpose in their flight.

In Kenya and Tanzania thousands of blue wildebeest and other animals migrate in herds to better grazing, covering more than a thousand kilometres without hesitation or resistance.

Ducks swim in an orderly and peacefully manner, usually in a row.

Society is, in a similar manner, characterised by normative rules which bring order to citizens' social and personal lives. If a person does not abide by rules and conventions, society has certain ways of dealing with social or criminal misconduct. It may be done through social sanctions or rejection, and in more serious cases legal instruments can be implemented.

It is always advisable to abide by or respect the normative practices of the society you are part of. These practices may be criticised in open societies.

Where unknown and foreign normative rules or patterns are followed, people have to be more diplomatic and refrain from indulging in public condemnation: Others' values must be respected.

Westerners may feel uncomfortable with the rigid and conservative social taboos that are honoured in Islamic societies. On the other hand, Muslims may feel uncomfortable in the open and free spheres of Western societies.

Norms include those actions which are desirable in a society, such as looking after old people. In Africa old-age homes are not well received, since it is the duty of children to look after their parents, and old people are highly respected.

In the words of Mandela, as noted above, the moral question is: "Can there be anything more important than looking after one's ageing mother?"

RELIGIOSITY

Religiosity is a reference of the degree to which people in a society are religious. It encompasses the belief in God, a Supreme Being, spirits and gods.

Religion has enormous power in the life experiences of people, and it supports the social values of communities. It gives meaning to life and develops life-coping abilities.

Africans are known to be extremely religious people, justifying the importance of the phenomenon of religiosity in all aspects of African life.

The importance of religiosity rests on the belief that there is a Supreme Being who has greater power than man. This Being is to be approached through ancestral spirits who are the communicators between man and the Being.

For example, the national anthem of South Africa, Nkosi Sikeleli iAfrika, is a religious composition meaning "God bless Africa". God is the equivalent of this Supreme Being.

Religiosity is regarded (Mokiti:1988:68) as the basis of Ubuntu culture and Africans believe that without God nothing will succeed in Africa. It has a deep concern about the fate of human beings, and religion forbids anti-Ubnuntu behaviour towards all others.

Belief in the ancestors and the power of the traditional sangomas (spiritual communicators) is still very strong, but the Christian and Muslim beliefs have become predominant in certain geographical areas of Africa. This predominant of other religions has created quite some confusion on how to accommodate these to co-exist with traditional beliefs.

For the purpose of this book, the point is that religion, in general, is of cardinal importance in the world views of Africans: All believe in some venerated form of a superior being.

APPRECIATION

To be appreciative is to be grateful.

Appreciation is an important skill needed to make up for shortcomings or to overcome obstacles in life. Nobody is perfect mentally or physically, yet there is always so much to be grateful for. An amputee still has another functioning limb, a person with diabetes probably does not endure the same level of pain as someone who is dying of cancer; an alcoholic can change his lifestyle and be respected again by refraining from drinking; an overweight person can lose weight by eating correctly and modestly, etc.

Many people accept basic life necessities like food, water and shelter as a given and do not show gratitude for having received these blessings.

Many people in Africa and other parts of the world make do without even these basic commodities.

Sometimes children do not eat because it is not their turn. Imagine not being able to eat when you are hungry, but due to the scarcity of food, you have to wait your turn to eat.

People's appreciation for human company is often re-evaluated when they lose loved ones who were once close to them, or are forced by circumstances to live solitary lives. When spending time in prison in complete isolation, a political prisoner (Mandela, op cit:322) realised that nothing "is more dehumanising than the absence of human companionship".

CONSIDERATION

Consideration is a skill that earns a person the respect of others.

Here the recommendation is that people cultivate attitudes which do not revolve around greed, and that they practise empathy.

Greed is negative. Greed is often the cause of financial malpractice and unhealthy competition where the idea is to gain the most and best at all costs. This leads to the exploitation of both humans and the environment.

Consideration for others fosters cooperative attitudes and peaceful coexistence.

 CHILDRENS RIGHTS

It is the duty of any government to protect the rights of its children. The Constitution of the Republic of South Africa states that children are entitled to the following: The right

- ➤ to be cared for, the right to food and the best possible healthcare, and the right to shelter
- ➤ to be educated
- ➤ to be proud of their culture and beliefs
- ➤ to special care (for children with disabilities)
- ➤ to be loved and protected from harm.

Legally, a child is defined as a young person under the age of 18 years. In South Africa offending children are referred to places of safety which are administered by the Department of Social Development, where they are instructed on topics like life skills, life-coping skills etc. Children are not sent to prison in cases of criminal misconduct, but are sentenced by courts to do community service. Usually children are then returned into the custody of their parents. (The policy of endeavouring to keep children out of prison is regulated by the Child Justice Bill as published in the Government Gazette No 23728 of 8 August 2002.)

Paragraph 16 of the Child Justice Bill states: "If a child cannot for any reason be released into the care of a parent or an appropriate adult or cannot be released on bail, the child must, in lieu of detention in police custody, be placed in a place of safety if such a place is available within a reasonable distance from the place where the child has to appear for a preliminary inquiry and there is a vacancy."

According to Conya Booyens, Chief Director of the section dealing with young offenders (children) in the institutions of the Gauteng Province, a total of 150 children were kept in prisons, compared to plus minus 900 children in the institutions of the Department of Social Development in the Gauteng province, during the first week of September 2006. Children in institutions have usually been involved in more minor offences like pick pocketing and housebreaking. In the institutions they are taught about life skills, life coping skills, values like Ubuntu values and the dangers of crime and social malpractices like substance abuse. This is a more human approach and children are not treated as prisoners.

CASE STUDY: THE LOBOLA ISSUE

Paying "lobola" (bride's gift, bride prize or dowry) is a highly respected custom whereby a bridegroom donates cows or money to his mother and father-in-law, as a token of his appreciation or as a gift to thank them for raising his bride-to-be.

The future groom normally pays lobola in the form of cattle to the groom's father. In modern times lobola can be paid in cash and payments can even be negotiated to be paid off in instalments!

If a man possesses enough cows and can afford to pay more lobola, it is an acceptable practice that such a person can marry more than one wife.

This case study is based on an actual encounter the author had with an old lady during a discussion at Shaka's Kraal, in Zululand.

Try to imagine a wealthy man with many cows who married seven women (under the lobola system, which allows him to be polygamous). The first wife felt that her husband did not respect her anymore, since he only paid attention to his youngest wife. The first wife became extremely depressed since she felt she was not being shown Ubuntu respect!

His chauvinistic behaviour was also not a sign of consideration and appreciation.

For discussion

Does the first woman have a valid reason for feeling depressed?

If the husband calls in his wives to discuss the matter, what should the resolution be to settle the issue harmoniously and respectfully?

Could you consider making up a play where the wives give their inputs, and see if there is a possible solution to this problem?

What is the lesson of this case study?

The Value of Compassion 7

"Umuntu ngbuntu ngabantu (I am because you are)"
  — *Ntate Kgalushi Drake Koka* (1996a:5)

INTRODUCTION

Compassion is about emotion.

Sharing emotive feelings with others includes rejoicing heartily with fellow men, or showing pity or mercy.

A true human being (the Ubuntu way) is to be human, to care, share, and respect others.

Compassionate people are warm and portray an image of being happy and enjoying life to the fullest. Enjoyment of life goes hand in hand with optimism and positivism. Compassion is regarded (Teffo, 1998:8) as an important value in African people's lives and it is particularly intense and prevalent in rural areas.

Ancient traditions are honoured in a passionate manner in most rural areas of Africa.

Rural people have been less influenced by Western values and still live according to original values, in the way in which they were taught.

Compassion is about reaching out to others.

Compassion is seen (Mangani, 1983:84) as that which humanism is all about: You are enlarged and enriched when you move beyond yourself.

Mangani declares: "I am attracted to an existence in which people treat each other as human beings and not simply as instruments and tools, where people become committed to each other without necessarily having to declare such commitment. When the chips are down it is compassion which makes it possible for other people to rise to the occasion. Compassion integrates and binds people together."

Compassion therefore relates to empathy or feeling for the suffering of others, prompting one to selflessly provide help to them, or to at least try to understand their sorrow or problems.

It is claimed (Du Preez, 1997:28) that according to the Ubuntu ethic the individual is encouraged to achieve, but never to the detriment of his fellow man. This is a reflection of compassion, since the dignity and humanness of the other person is taken into account at all times, and even regarded as a higher priority than one's own situation.

Compassion is evident in traditional, warm and all-embracing community life.

Socialising informally and heartily is a key element of African life: The challenge is for all people of the world to become likewise happy and friendly, informal human beings.

The isiZulu word for the enquiry "How are you?" is "Unjane?" in the single form and "Ninjane?" in the plural. One often finds that the word "Ninjane" is used even when the enquiry refers to the well-being of a single person. The reason for this is that in Africa one does not enquire about the good or bad luck of a single person only, but about the well-being of all those related or connected to a person (for instance his spouse, friends, children and the rest of his extended family). In Kenya, this type of enquiry includes the well-being of the person's cows!

Greeting is a timeous process and indicates compassionate respect for other human beings.

Handshakes are often performed in a three-step process which is symbolic for person A asking how B is, B responding that he is fine, before A confirms that he is also well. People tend to keep holding hands for quite a while, to foster a spirit of warmth and compassion for each other. Men are often seen walking hand in hand – not because of homosexual tendencies, but to illustrate their comradeship or companionship.

Compassion in the life of Africans manifests in different events, conventions, rituals and codes of behaviour. These conventions are (in many respects) contrary to the conventions and habits of Westerners.

CULTURAL DIFFERENCES AS REGARDS COMPASSION

Examples of differences in compassion between African and Western or European cultures, are as follows (Broodryk, 2002, op cit:62):

EVENT	AFRICAN	WESTERN
Baby sleeping	Abba (the child is carried on the mother's back)	Cot
Baby feeding	Breast-feeding	Bottle-feeding
Punishment	Verbal	Corporal

Event	African	Western
Marriage	Ubuntu norm (lobola: rewarding the parents-in-law)	Class snobs
Family	Extended (many fathers and mothers)	Nuclear
Elders	Part of family (sages)	Old-age homes
Death	No hell, the dead move into world of ancestors	Heaven or hell
Burials	Mass community participation	Private
Ancestors	Present, honoured	Hereafter
Medical	Sangomas	Doctors (person-centred treatment) (symptom)
Education	Initiation students	School pupils
Greeting	Informal, inquisitive	Formal, to the point
Laughter	Uninhibited, loud	Inhibited, happily grinning
Respect	Communal obedience	Individual conscience
Lifestyle	Spontaneity, informality	Reserved, formal

EVENT	AFRICAN	WESTERN
Relations	Open, heartily warm	Closed, lukewarm
Time concept	Tolerant, non-punctual	Rigid punctuality

LOVE

The appreciation of love is fundamental to the Ubuntu way of life.

It is amazing how happiness is reflected when children are brought up in an atmosphere of love and compassion. Such children usually live according to the values discussed earlier: They are kind, forgiving, empathic and sympathetic.

Africans show compassion for others. Showing love has dramatic results: It immediately brings a feeling of warmth to any environment.

Coupled with the value of loving, is the value of happiness. Love should always be a happy experience and in this way, they will also experience a greater sense of meaning in life. Love is not jealous. Love forgives and endures. It fosters happy attitudes and a positive acceptance of whatever events come your way in life.

Oduro (op cit:2) found in research done in Ghana that the first and most basic need of children was merely to receive love from their parents. This is the very first requirement for successful parenting, and also a crucial parenting skill: So simple, yet so applicable. Love your children – after all, they did not ask to be here.

Muslims advocate peace and love as the basic tenets of their religion.

The Christian religion couples love (Bible, New Testament, Romans 12:9) with various other Ubuntu life-coping values:

"Love must be sincere."

"Hate what is evil and cling to the good. Be devoted to one another in brotherly love. Honour one another above yourselves. Never be lacking in zeal, but keep your spiritual fervour, serving the Lord."

"Be joyful in hope, patient in affliction, faithful in prayer. Share with God's people who are in need."

"Bless those who persecute you; bless and do not curse. Rejoice with those who rejoice; mourn with those who mourn."

"Live in harmony with one another."

"Do not be proud, but be willing to associate with people of lowly position..."

Love is therefore an important life-coping skill and everyone should endeavour to be open to loving thoughts and the good things in life. The trick is to continuously fill the mind with positive thoughts, and to close the mind off to all that is evil, bad, vulgar or causes worry, anxiety and fear.

COHESION

Cohesion is the feeling of belonging and spiritually experiencing the so-called esprit de corps of a group or family. It manifests in intimate teamwork and loyalty, as well as commitment. The skill of establishing a sense of cohesion with respected or loved ones enriches the life activities of all concerned. It provides a sense of living happily and meaningfully.

INFORMALITY

People from closed societies or surroundings usually have hordes of taboos and prohibitions that make their personal lives unbearable and miserable.

In an open society or environment space is maintained for individuals to explore life in all its variety.

In Africa people live informally. Their less inhibited lifestyle encourages informality and easy living. Informality is visible in relaxed or friendly chatting, behaviour and thought. Informality is a natural way of enjoying life.

FORGIVENESS

To forgive is said to be divine. This is a popular notion which is seldom observed in practice.

In Africa forgiveness is a reality in the sense that Africans are generally quick to forgive. One example of this (and one which has already been referred to) was the forgiving attitude Nelson Mandela portrayed on being released from prison. He showed no signs of bitterness and hatred after being imprisoned for 27 years as an anti-apartheid activist. He could have chosen to take the route of facilitating a bloody revolution. Instead he involved himself in peaceful negotiations. This gesture of human forgiveness is illustrative of Mandela's stature as being the personification of the Ubuntu lifestyle.

It is common practice in certain working environments, like in the military milieu, to reprimand people severely when they make mistakes, and treat them as if they are slaves – transgressions are not tolerated.

The paradigm shift which needs to be made in the work and life environment, is to embrace your mistakes: It is alright to make mistakes. It is common knowledge that nobody likes to be in the wrong, and the Ubuntu guideline is to learn from your mistakes for they are (and should be seen as) part of the learning process.

This lesson is extremely important where new and inexperienced employees enter the workplace. Know that they will make mistakes, but assist them in a human manner and encourage them not to repeat these mistakes.

Everyone makes mistakes, but mistakes could be valuable life lessons, and it is only through erring that most people learn.

If people do make mistakes they should be forgiven, and if someone is rude, try to see his or her behaviour in perspective by being empathic. In other words, put yourself in their position or predicament and think of a possible reason for this type of behaviour. This may help you understand this unacceptable yet forgivable behaviour.

SPONTANEITY

Ubuntu people in most parts of Africa commonly practise the skill of being spontaneous.
Spontaneity is a natural response of carefree and (almost) stress-free living.

Being addicted to good cheer is a positive addiction. It is a tonic to associate with people of good cheer, because cheerfulness breeds further cheerfulness.

Ubuntu personalities are characterised by their spontaneous behaviour.

KINDNESS

Kindness is a human virtue. It encompasses those qualities in another person which are nice or commendable. Nice people are kind people and kind people are nice people.

Kind people, like nice people, stand out in a crowd. It is amazing how people who are kind and friendly, are respected by others. In a roomful of people, the whole mood changes when a kind person enters. It is as if a warm and kind personality affects everyone he or she comes into contact with.

In the competitive world people fail to live up to the expectations of kindness because of urgent obligations and time constraints: Shopping must be done, meetings must be attended as a rigid punctual convention, etc. leaving them very little room to practise kindness as well.

The Ubuntu way of approaching daily life is to be friendly, positive and accommodating. Nice people attract other nice people.

In this regard the Law of Attraction describes (Bremer,1980:201) the human approach to others. The Law is based on the notion that like produces like. "Plus" thoughts build; "minus" and negative thoughts tear down. One builds and grows as one thinks. Whatever one asserts, or firmly believes, one tends to become. As positive people are attracted to each other, negative people are similarly attracted to each other.

Kind people therefore will also tend to be attracted to other kind people.

CASE STUDY:
APPLICATION OF COMPASSIONATE VALUES

Cultural philosopher Credo Mutwa, in an address to media on the lack of society's expression of compassion to children, said (Tintinger, 1999:11) inter alia:

"Our children become criminals not so much because of poverty but because they have never been given a chance to know themselves, and who they are, because self-knowledge is the key to reform and the key to all civilisations.

"Our society is failing our children. We, the parents, are letting our children down, we the parents are failing in our most sacred duty, to see to it that our children grow up into men and women, creative and far-sighted people, and not monsters that will afterwards kill us, their parents."

"Today we do not reward our children, today we do not praise our children. I say let us change our approach to our children, let us heal more and punish less."

"I say to all of us, let us pray together. I say to all of us, let us weep together. I say to all of us, let us work together."

For discussion

How can the compassionate values of love, cohesion, informality, forgiveness, spontaneity and kindness be of assistance in raising positive children?

The Practical Living of Ubuntu Values

8

"Life in Alexandra was exhilarating and precarious. Its atmosphere was alive, its spirit adventurous, its people resourceful...I always regarded Alexandra Township as a home where I had no specific house, and Orlando as a place where I had a house but no home."

— *Nelson Mandela* (op cit:71)

TRADITIONAL LIFE

Ubuntu has always been part and parcel of traditional African life.

The values of Ubuntu were transferred from generation to generation in a narrative way.

Mandela (op cit:11) recalls that his father would tell stories about historic battles and heroic Xhosa warriors whilst his mother would enchant the children with Xhosa legend and fables that had come down through countless generations. These tales stimulated the imagination of the children, and usually contained some moral or Ubuntu lesson.

In this way people's lives were shaped by moral lessons, customs, rituals and taboos. That was the alpha and omega of existence. Men followed the path laid out for them by their fathers and women led the same lives as their mothers before them.

Details of these stories were remembered in full detail.

Traditional African societies placed a high value on human worth. It was humanism that found its expression in a communal context rather than in individualism, which is prominent in Western lifestyles.

The difference between the African and Western life approaches is based on the "we" (African inclusiveness) versus the "I" (Western exclusiveness) styles. In Africa, group spirit is regarded as more valuable than individual aspirations. This explains the collective spirit or brotherhood of Africans.

Ubuntu captures the essence of this particular participatory humanism and is visible today in the communal and collective spirit of the ghetto townships, where people stand together to overcome hunger and poverty.

In such a communal spirit everyone is part of an extended family and there are no social classes to be found based on materialistic assets: All share the assets, food and drinks.

In African culture, the sons and daughters of one's aunts and uncles are considered and respected as brothers and sisters. The uncles and aunts are also regarded as fathers and mothers. There are no half-brothers or half-sisters, nephews or nieces – they are all part of an extended family. One also finds no orphans: If the natural parents of a child die, the care of that person is automatically taken over by the other uncles or aunts as co-parents.

Mandela (op cit:112) remembers that he found himself strongly drawn to the idea of a classless society which, to his mind, was similar to traditional African culture where life was shared and communal.

Westerners are seemingly inclined to be less sharing when it comes to underprivileged people. Sparks (op cit:42) regards Ubuntu as a subtle concept which is not easily translatable to Westerners.

Ubuntu broadly means that each individual's humanity is ideally expressed through his relationship with others, and theirs in turn through a recognition of his humanity. As human beings, all are equal.

In general Westerners do not regard all civilisations as equal, and distinguish between first, second and third worlds. This viewpoint indicates that the more materially successful Western societies are of a higher developed class (first world), and African societies of an inferior and less-developed nature (third world). Humanism in African countries is not considered a valuable criterion for determining the degree of civilisation.

The criterion for these distinctions is thus based on material considerations, not human considerations.

In traditional Ubuntu daily living the emphasis was based on human considerations. The living of human Ubuntu values manifested in African life through various activities and ceremonies.

Various examples of such events are found (Broodryk 2002, op cit:62) in: The sharing of whatever one has with others in the community and not in self-enrichment, in simple conventions like when mothers carry babies on their back in warm blankets instead of using a baby cot (they "abba" them), practising breast-feeding instead of feeding with milk bottles, respecting uncles and aunts like one's own fathers or mothers instead of keeping your distance, and keeping elders inside the caring extended family system instead of abandoning them into old-age homes.

In interacting with others one finds Ubuntu people distinguishing themselves from other cultures in the way they greet (heartily, hugging), mix (socialising with all, bosses and workers on equal basis), spontaneous dancing whenever a musical beat is heard or good news is received, talking and laughing loudly coupled with vibrant body language. The custom was to eat with one's hands (historically knives and forks were unknown), to drink beer from a calabash (huge communal mug made from clay), to relax with songs and play self-made drums was customary, religious beliefs were often praised and popularised through hymns and it is still not strange to hear Africans humming religious songs. Where there is joy, celebrations play an important role in rewarding the cause of the joy. All were invited, and music was the mystical methodology which gave manifestation to messages of the mind and heart (Africans are emotive human beings and this often reflects in their music and songs).

Music is described (Ramose, op cit: 59) as the conception and harmony of be-ing in African philosophy. The dance of be-ing is an invitation to participate actively in and through the music of be-ing rather than being a passive spectator thereof. This explains the difference in both attitude and reaction towards music (the dance of be-ing) between Africans and non-Africans: One does not listen to music seated!

Traditionally Africans lived from day to day, from daybreak until evening. Work and play lasted from sunrise to sunset. During the evenings people would dance, eat, drink, rejoice or tell stories around the magical African fire. Time was a plenty and not measured by wrist watches or time clocks.

Modern Living

These manifestations of Ubuntu living and the validity of moral stories are applicable in modern environments. Mandela remembers (op cit:11) a story told by his mother, which is still of value today.

The story is about a travelling visitor who was approached by an old woman with terrible cataracts in her eyes. When the woman asked the traveller for help, the man adverted his eyes.

Then another man came along and was approached by the same old woman. She asked him to clean her eyes and even though he found the task unpleasant, he did as asked. Then, miraculously, the scales fell from the old woman's eyes and she became young and beautiful. The man married her and became wealthy and prosperous. It is a simple tale but the message is an enduring one: Virtue and generosity will be rewarded in ways one that one cannot know.

In modern times it is advisable to recognis virtues make one's self-coping efforts easier.

This is a reference to self-management as an important life-coping skill. Self-management takes place in physical, institutional, economical and social environments.

"Physical environment" refers to the home one lives in, the workplace, churches, roads, and general infrastructures. A home in an informal settlement or squatter camp can evoke negative experiences of depression or misery and dampen someone's mood.

"Institutional environment" is about politics and policies and the execution thereof, which may directly influence the life of a person. A policy may favour certain races or tribes.

The "economic environment" may be influenced by a shortage of resources, which leads to a scarcity of money. Not having money available has drastic consequences. A beggar undergoes the humiliating experience of being scaled down to his begging role.

"Social environment" refer to the activities of social institutions like churches and welfare organisations. A faith may have certain absolute dogmas which interfere with the freedoms and activities of their adherents.

These four environments can be compared with the four teats of a cow to give it a more African flavour. A cow is an important phenomenon even in modern African life.

Cows can have an economic impact, for example, where a future bride's parents are rewarded with cows (the lobola system of marriage or bridal gifts). The number of cows one possesses still determines one's wealth in many communities.

Cattle are slaughtered at funerals to feed those from far away – this tradition is still followed.

Cows are respected. Prior to the slaughtering, communication traditionally takes place with the cow to apologise for slaughter. An explanation will also be given for this fatal event. This situation is still largely applicable.

It would therefore be appropriate to refer to the management or life skills process (in an Ubuntu sense) in the context of a cow, and especially the four teats of a cow.

The teats of a cow have as their function the provision of milk. The activity of milking the cow may be compared with output or productivity, and the product, (the milk) is the outcome of the whole process. The teats are usually milked in a certain order and style, and all four are used in this process. Milk is obtained for human consumption purposes or economical motives (selling the milk to generate profit).

Self-management may likewise be compared to the act of milking a cow.

Management functions have a "leadership teat", a "social environment teat", a "cultural teat" and a "strategy teat". These functions are usually also performed in a certain order, starting with self-leadership (being in control), an analysis of the social environment (physical, religious or other factors limiting freedom of thought and behaviour), cultural taboos (the conventions and accepted ways of behaviour), and a strategy to cope with life in a variety of environments.

In both traditional and modern life ancestors are acknowledged or still recognised as the living dead, meaning that they are not forgotten. The ancestors are experienced as being present in all people's daily lives. Ancestors also remain part of the family and community and are forever remembered by the family, especially at special occasions and ritual events.

In community life, when people are enjoying themselves around a calabash of beer, one may find that a little bit of beer is poured on the ground for the ancestors to enjoy. They are especially honoured at community mealtime events or during offerings and sacrifices.

An example hereof was a very special event organised by the jazz legend Jonas Gwangwa and his wife Violet. They travelled the world and met years ago when both were living abroad "in exile" (they voluntarily lived outside South Africa during the apartheid years).

They still honour their traditional beliefs in the ancestors and in July 2006 they held a traditional ceremony at theirhome in Observatory, Jo'burg, to thank the ancestors for bringing the Gwangwa and Nalatleng (Violet's maiden name) families together. They slaughtered sheep, brewed traditional beer, and spoilt the gathered family and friends with an unforgettable feast.

Many Africans believe in God through the ancestors as mediums. God is experienced as being very far away, whilst the ancestors are here in the midst of ordinary people.

The belief in the existence of ancestors should not though be regarded as unique or strange. As Khoza (1994:89) puts it: " Nobody has the right to say I am barbaric because I believe in the dead, particularly when they themselves believe in Isaiah and Abraham" (Biblical figures who were also regarded as ancestors).

In general, it appears as if the living dead in African family life are finally forgotten after five or six generations, but they are still honoured as being with the living for all eternity. On the eternal vibe they become part of the spiritual world. There is therefore no heaven or hell awaiting them. They will merely join the world of spirits, becoming spirits themselves. In the spiritual world there is unique communication between ancestors and sangomas.

Spirits can possess living human beings. An example is provided (Motshekga, 1988:155) of where an accused was charged with two accounts of murder and wrongfully viewed by the court as insane.

The accused, in accordance with African thought, could not be regarded as insane but should rather have been appreciated as being possessed by an ancestral spirit, which could have been allowed to settle and serve as a guardian spirit.

Detaining spirit-possessed people in Western mental institutions is also incomprehensible, because they cannot cure a spirit-possessed person – it is the sangoma's task to cure the affected person. Due to the sangomas' psychic training and experience of ancestral spirits as well as their own purification, they have learnt to "see" and not just to observe. "Seeing" implies moving beyond ordinary sensory perception and understanding. Sangomas regard themselves as being engaged in a war of good against the evil forces in nature.

LIFE DURING THE APARTHEID ERA

In the period between the traditional and the modern era, colonialisation took place when European countries like Britain, Portugal, the Netherlands and Germany took possession of various African countries.

In South Africa colonisation led to the creation and maintenance of laws and regulations restricting the life of black people in a dramatic way. These restrictions had negative influences on the whay of life of black Africans.

These restrictions included petty measures to make life unbearable for black people.

Examples of apartheid measures were:

➢ The Group Areas Act determined where people were supposed to live: Black people were regarded as temporary citizens and were not allowed to own houses or land.

➢ Black, coloured and Indian people were segregated from white areas and forced to live apart.

➢ If land (occupied by the afore mentioned non-white groups) was needed for the expansion of white housing or development, the inhabitants were forcefully removed from the occupied land.

➢ Black people were not allowed in cinemas, churches, schools, institutions, parks, restaurants, post offices, on beaches or in pubs situated in so-called white areas.

➢ Mixed marriages and relationships between blacks and whites were prohibited by law.

➢ Multi-racial sport and social mixing were not allowed between the different races.

➢ Black people could not consume alcohol legally.

➢ Black people were not accommodated in the civil service.

➢ Black people could not be buried in the same cemetaries as white people.

➢ In the Free State an ordinance prohibited black people from walking on pavements, and Indians could spend a maximum of one day in the province.

➢ Black students were compelled to enrol for the white language of Afrikaans and

➢ Black people were prohibited ffrom participating in politics: The first democratic national election only took place in 1994.

It was only due to the Ubuntu life-coping skills of tolerance, peace, and forgiveness that South Africa never experienced a true bloody revolution. This statement is confirmed by Shutte (op cit:33) and Asmal (2001: letter).

According to Shutte non-violent revolution in South Africa was not possible since those who had been depressed for so long by the apartheid regime practised the life-coping skill of Ubuntu. The real miracle was the survival of Ubuntu on such a mammoth scale. Extraordinary manifestations of the forgiveness facets of Ubuntu during the hearings of the Truth and Reconciliation Commission were something unique in the history of mankind. During these hearings the most gruesome and depressing evidence was delivered about serious malpractices executed by the apartheid minority apartheid regime and its security forces against the opponents of the apartheid system.

In a letter to the author, a former Minister of Education, Prof Kader Asmal, states that it was due to Ubuntu that a bloody revolution never took place. Ubuntu now forms the basis of the national education values, thereby ensuring a more ordered and human society for the future.

It was only after the abolition of apartheid that life in South Africa returned to normal.

MORAL REGENERATION

Conduct in the spirit of integrity and transparency are important pillars in the Ubuntu way of life. In recent times there has been renewed interest in incorporating Ubuntu values into people's daily and professional conduct.

The establishment of the Moral Regeneration Movement was preceded by the development of the Ubuntu Code of Conduct and the Ubuntu Pledge.

On 23 October 1998 all political parties represented in the Parliament of the Republic of South Africa (with the exception of only one small white right wing party) accepted a Code of Conduct based on the values of Ubuntu, for persons in positions of responsibility.

As a preamble it was stated that all persons in positions of responsibility have a duty to serve the people of South Africa with integrity.

These include elected representatives of the people, officers of the government in the legislatures and public service, and those with authority in political, economic and civil organisations.

This noble obligation is reflected in the principles of integrity, incorruptibility, good faith, impartiality, openness, accountability, justice, generosity, respect and leadership.

The Code of Conduct for people in positions of responsibility, was followed by the Ubuntu Pledge.

Ancient Ubuntu principles portrayed in the religious-ethical Pledge of Ubuntu include: To be good and do well, to live honestly and positively, to be considerate and kind, to care for sisters and brothers within the human family, to respect other people's rights to their beliefs and cultures, to care for and improve the environment, to promote peace, harmony and non-violence, and to promote the welfare of South Africa as a patriotic citizen.

A historic event for the acknowledgement of Ubuntu took place on 18 March 2002, when delegates who had signed and supported the Ubuntu Pledge met at a workshop focusing on how to implement the Pledge. This led to the establishment of the Moral Regeneration Movement.

The movement opened offices in Jo'burg. It has as its goal to have all education authorities subscribing to the following positive Ubuntu values: To

➤ respect human dignity and values

➤ promote freedom, the Rule of Law and democracy

➤ improve material well-being and economic justice

➤ enhance family and community values

➤ uphold loyalty, honesty and integrity

➤ ensure harmony in culture, belief and conscience

➤ show respect and concern for all people

➤ strive for justice, fairness and peaceful co-existence.

If all people can subscribe to the living of these values, a new moral order will globally be created, thus making coping with life more simple and pleasant.

Internationally, the challenge is to have this movement of propagating positive moral behaviour, replicated all over.

CASE STUDY:
APPLICATION OF UBUNTU IN PRACTICAL LIFE

The issue is whether there is a real universal similarity between Ubuntu/African practical living and other cultures of the world. In other words, is Ubuntu life unique to Africa, or is it universal and therefore applicable to all cultures?

Do you agree or disagree with the statement that it is evident from the above that there are different and opposing ways of living (African and Western societies), but that all basic values are universal?

Do you agree that the Ubuntu lifestyle appears to be more human, more caring and sharing than most of the lifestyles globally, especially because of the intensity factor and warmth of Ubuntu living?

The crucial question is: If the African or Ubuntu lifestyle is more attractive from a human perspective, should not all of us strive to become more natural, friendly, intensely caring human beings and structure our behaviour and cultures accordingly?

How is this to be done in your specific situation, namely in your family set up, workplace, university or school environment?

Ubuntu Self-Motivation

"An unexamined life is not worth living."

Socrates (469-399 B.C.)

INTRODUCTION

As a case study, discuss the following incident (Diescho, 1993: UNISA): A young boy went to the river to have a swim. He undressed and dived into the water naked.

Then a second young boy came along and being in a naughty mood, took the first boy's clothes and started running away with them. Consequently the first boy jumped out of the water naked to chase the second boy.

There were two onlookers or observers sitting on a hill nearby. They only saw the naked boy running, whereupon the first observer exclaimed in a laughing manner: "Ha ha ha, look at that boy! HE IS STREAKING!!!" The second observer, however, looked concerned and commented: "Shame, I wonder what happened to him?"

It is clear that the second onlooker reflected a caring and Ubuntu approach.

Do you agree?

It is claimed (Rogers, 1995:484) that at one time or another every individual asks himself or herself – sometimes calmly and meditatively, sometimes in agonising uncertainty or despair – the following age-old questions:

What is my goal in life?
What am I striving for?
What is my purpose?

These are cardinal questions.

Everyone should regularly examine whether their life has any worth. If there is the slightest doubt about your purpose, goal or vision in life, it is time to analyse yourself, and to motivate yourself to tackle life with renewed zeal.

This chapter aims to help readers with self-motivation.

Ubuntu self-motivation is philosophical, since it encourages a person to seek understanding and meaning in life.

Introspection is about obtaining wisdom about yourself. Introspection leads to self-counselling.

Self-counselling and motivation are not in competition with the other disciplines in counselling, since their focus is on obtaining clarification and some perspective of certain issues in your life, by applying the necessary guidelines as provided in this chapter.

Self-clarification is reached after you have analysed the meaning of your own situation for yourself. Through analysis, you create a new direction for yourself, or go about discovering or rediscovering your own life vision: It is a self-help exercise.

You, as an individual – without the guidance of an outside counsellor – make this discovery.

Self-motivation does not focus on healing a patient, but on the self-explanation, clarification and self-invention of a normal and healthy person.

It is African in the sense that it approaches a person as a human being and as a totality, as practised by sangomas (African psychologists) and sages (wise people).

It is therefore not only one isolated action or symptom (as expressed by the individual) which qualifies for attention, but the whole being in a holistic way.

Ubuntu self-motivation is a therapeutic method for a happier or healthier life. It includes questions on the meaning of life, why you are alive, and how to arrive at the best way of living (finding the greatest qualitative happiness in life).

The abovementioned methodology can also be applied to groups of people, and even to organisations as part of motivational or directional experiments. It will be advisable, though, for a trained philosophical counsellor to assist such groups.

The reason for this statement is that philosophical counselling is relatively new and only a handful of trained philosophical counsellors are now practising in South Africa and some other countries like the US and the Netherlands. Untrained counsellors without recent philosophical qualifications will not have acquired the necessary philosophical skills to help give birth (like a midwife) to ideas on the exact meaning of issues concerned, or to find solutions through Socratic and African suspicion and investigation.

The background of philosophical counselling dates back to the era of Socrates. The Socratic method was based primarily on investigative questioning regarding the meaning of concepts.

It is a reference to the methodology used by the philosopher Socrates (469-399 BC). Very little information is available about Socrates except for descriptions of him – none of his writings have survived. Socrates, according to the philosopher Plato, concerned himself with the nature of virtue. Virtue was seen as knowledge and Socrates was known to study a particular virtue and question its meaning.

It is claimed (Nemavhandu, op cit:2) that black Egyptians priests taught African philosophy to the best minds in Greece – people like Plato, Thales, Aristotle, Democritus, Anaximander and others (according to this source one of the sculptures of Socrates clearly shows that he was an African).

By understanding ancient Ubuntu as a world view and an African philosophy, and investigating its influence on different environments and cultural aspects (as discussed in previous chapters), anyone can start working on a Socratic methodology to arrive at the meaning of his or her own life, and to become self-motivated.

This can also be done in conjunction with other caring persons. Traditional African beliefs are more concerned with the collective interests of the group than with those of an individual.

Mbiti (1996:108) explains the collective approach of an African person as follows: "When he suffers, he does not suffer alone but with the corporate group. When he rejoices, he rejoices not alone but with his kinsmen, his neighbours and his relatives, whether dead or living. Whatever happens to the individual happens to the whole group, and whatever happens to the whole group happens to the individual. The individual can only say: I am, because we are; and since we are, I am".

As a result of this view, self-motivation should make provision for the inclusion of others, like relatives, if required.

The same aforementioned procedure basically applies to any individual or group exercises.

SELF-MOTIVATION METHODOLOGY

The self-motivation strategy can be divided into five basic steps:

Firstly, the genuine problem(s) or issue(s) has to be identified and isolated. The best word to describe the situation has to be explored thoroughly. The true meaning of the word has to be analysed and made applicable to the problematic situation. Is this really the best description for the dilemma?

The focus is on a form of suspicion and doubt: You wonder, and question.

It may be helpful to list words as either "obstacles" or "worries" and to do so under separate headings. The difference is that obstacles could be of such a serious nature that they cannot be overcome, while worries are just negative thoughts or assumptions.

The second step is to formulate a vision (a dream, or an ideal situation without the problem or issue, i.e. the problem has been eliminated). A vision should be practical and attainable. The importance of a vision lies in its value as direction-giver.

A vision should be revisited continuously and constantly redefined once it has been realised. The aim of formulating a vision is to provide greater meaning and sense to the existence of a person or organisation.

The third step is to compile a mission (the "How?" statement or method). Resources which are available have to be identified and utilised fully. They could include human allies, physical objects and even abstract phenomena. The latter could include religious beliefs (like one finds amongst certain tribes in New Zealand) and conventions or communication with ancestors (as experienced with Africans).

The fourth step is to develop an integrated "Obstacles, Negatives, Positives and Outcomes" (ONPO) analysis as regards the internal and external situations. This integrated approach allows for greater freedom of thought, since there are no limitations in the space of thinking: There are no restrictions to the rational planning process.

The fifth step follows after allocating these generated ideas and putting them in perspective. Now a personal action plan has to be developed by the individual himself. The person decides what to do, how to do it and who else he is going to rely on as a human resource in accordance with the action programme.

It is essential that the programme and action plans be implemented within specific time frames and that regular evaluation and monitoring or after-care be done.

IDENTIFYING THE PROBLEMATIC ISSUE

The author has identified various words to describe a variety of conditions occurring in human life.

The challenge is to determine which words most accurately describe the problematic situation.

As a first step, a maximum of five words which are indicative of your dilemma, have to be identified from this batch of words (see page 107), and the meaning of each word has to be thoroughly understood (to ensure that the words are in fact descriptive of the problem or situation).

The second step is to prioritise these five words from one to five, in order to determine which single word captures the main issue or best describes the problem.

The third step is to use this specifically identified word or concept as the focal point for in-depth thinking. This suspicious consideration of the concept will help transform the problem into an outcome or solution, in the form of a new vision which is applicable to the person or group.

To implement the first step, the descriptive words are offered herewith, and the five words best describing the person's position can now be identified.

Words to choose from, to best describe one's personal dilemma or emotional state:

aggression	ailment	angry
apathy	break away	blame
bored	burdened	chest pains
closed	confession	concern
confusion	crazy	dead
darkness	defenceless	demonic
depressed	dissatisfied	disillusioned
despondence	dejected	destroyed
despair	dismayed	discouraged
disgrace	doubtful	drug-addict
dull	emotional	endogenic
exposed	frustrated	gloomy
heartache	hateful	hallucinating
helpless	hopeless	horny
hypertension	hurried	humiliated
hurt	impotent	inferior
innocent	incurable	insensitive
incomprehension	insomniac	insulted
irrelevant	irritable	lacking in confidence
lazy	lost	loss
lonely	low self-esteem	lunatic
manic	melancholy	miserable

depressed	devilish	disillusioned
negativism	neurotic	nothingness
overweight	oversensitive	pained
panicky	pessimistic	phobic
plodding	poor	rejected
restless	rotten	sad
sceptical	self-examination	self pitying
senseless	short of breath	tiresome
tired of life	torn	unemployed
ugly	useless	ungrateful
uninspired	undecided	impersonal
unhappy	unreliable	unpleasant
uninterested	unintelligent	unstable
unsympathetic	unsure	
worthless		

Knowing which words have been chosen, the self-motivator should now question whether the identified words actually best describe the problem or situation, and if that is not the case, to decide on the word which does.

From the original five words, a single word is selected for further investigation.

The person now has to formulate an ideal situation which is a positive response to the negative word identified. Knowing and understanding what the main problem is, the person should now think creatively about possible ideal scenarios (not solutions) to nullify the problem.

From these a single scenario (vision) is to be selected as the ideal situation.

FORMULATING A PERSONAL VISION

A vision can be applicable to an individual, organisation or society.

One often hears politicians talking about their vision or dream for the nation. Care should be taken not to simplify visions and dreams. If a politician spends every moment of the day dreaming, that constitutes daydreaming – it is not visionary dreaming.

The vision should be to become a happier, less stressed, more human, caring, sharing, respectful and compassionate person, enjoying a quality life to the full.

Before you can arrive at the vision, a mission has to be compiled. The mission is the vehicle that will take you to your destination.

DEFINING A PERSONAL MISSION

The mutual mission of a group could be to determine how they will use an Ubuntu way to arrive at their formulated vision. For instance, through intensive and continuous discussions and, the committed implementation of identified activities, followed by further consultation and progress evaluations.

The mission of the individual is to define his vision (i.e. his personal dream), to determine the status quo, his own immediate surroundings and milieu or problematic situation, and thereafter to work on a very practical plan of action for his present and future life (the past is dead and gone).

A practical programme or plan of action is therefore the way forward after doing an in-depth analysis of the self. This programme of action is the roadmap which will determine how and when you arrive at your chosen destination.

USING A PERSONAL ONPO-ANALYSIS

The ONPO analysis has been referred (Broodryk, 2005:147) to in its applicability to management philosophy.

In this book the ONPO analysis is applied to the individual's predicament in coping with the obstacles of life.

The ONPO (Obstacles, Negatives, Positives, and Outcomes) analysis is holistic and does not differentiate between internal and external influences like the SWOT (Strengths, Weaknesses, Opportunities and Threats) analysis does.

The SWOT analysis is mainly applicable to organisational structures and was not originally designed to help those struggling with problems in life, work and their environment.

The ONPO analysis is therefore offered as an alternative to the SWOT analysis when it comes to solving both human problems and organisational issues. The ONPO analysis is inclusively based on an integrated external and internal investigation of all four elements.

This human application is a form of philosophical counselling, which springs from the conviction that human beings are responsible for finding their own solutions to problems or issues. This can be done through the ONPO analysis.

One example of an obstacle (from an Ubuntu perspective) in the life of any society, is migration: People from rural areas migrate to urban areas where they lose their basic Ubuntu values while living in abject social conditions. A poor and miserable environment tends to influence social discipline negatively.

For the individual a broken marriage could be an obstacle, as could the loss of a job or a loved one.

Negatives are "softer" obstacles. They are not as dominant and may relatively easily be transformed into positives.

One example of a negative (in the context of an Ubuntu society) is the reluctance with which people approach changes which were designed to bring about a better life or situation.

For the individual a negative could be feelings of sadness or misery.

It is relatively easy to transform negatives into positives, and occasionally all that is needed is a change of mindset and subsequent action.

Positives, in an Ubuntu context, are the need to revive Ubuntu to create a happy and peaceful society, the fact that Ubuntu is the business philosophy of various companies, and the implementation of Ubuntu in government structures and policies.

For an individual, a positive could be that there are training opportunities to hone one's own job skills, or that there are caring family members available to provide emotional support when needed.

Outcomes are opportunities derived from obstacles.

In an Ubuntu society, as mentioned above, the obstacle of migration would decline because Ubuntu is less threatened. This implies a revival of Ubuntu values where they have been lost. An example of such a revival is the process of moral regeneration.

Africans may see Western domination as an obstacle to living in Africa. Western influences, as obstacles, may on the other hand be seen as transformed Outcomes for the acceptance of Ubuntu as world view globally, since humanism (which is the basis of Ubuntu) is a universal, global value.

Critical, logical analysis by Western academics on Ubuntu philosophy becomes less relevant if one regards Ubuntu as a highly respected, emotive African world view, which is less concerned with cold, rational thinking.

Ubuntu is regarded as possessing something of the sacred, and is therefore part of a different academic approach.

Ubuntu is emotive and deals with a world view which has – for centuries – been passed down through generations.

Obstacles can be changed into opportunities through a change in mindset. If someone else's resistance is an obstacle, it could become an exciting challenge to break that very resistance: When the going gets tough, the tough get going.

After the ONPO planning session has been completed, a personal action programme with realistic timeframes should be added, implemented and continuously evaluated.

DEVELOPING
A PERSONAL ACTION PLAN

The ideas that flow from the ONPO analysis can be used for the development of a comprehensive personal action programme or plan, under the following headings:

The problem(s) as identified above (description)

The cause of the problem (origin)

The solution to the problem (vision)

The activity needed to solve the problem (mission)

Who is doing what (actor) in this process

When is the activity to take place (time frame).

A heading entitled "Check" must be added to the plan, in order to monitor whether the activities were completed within the time frame.

Personal Action Programme

Problem	Cause	Solution	Activity	Doer	Time	Check
What?	Why?	How?	What?	Who?	When?	Done?

Exercise:
Alcoholic-to-be

A man studied the descriptive words (see p107) to arrive at a description of his own personal dilemma.

He decided that the word "depressed" best described his dilemma. He realised that the reason for his depression was a problem he had developed with alcohol, due to loneliness after the tragic death of his beloved wife.

He decided that his vision was to become sober again.

His mission was to stop drinking alcohol, to socialise more often and in so-doing to combat his loneliness. He did the ONPO analysis as a brainstorming exercise and found that loneliness was his major obstacle.

The negative which flowed from this was his excessive drinking aimed at passing time. The positive solution for this negative (drinking) was to drink fewer alcoholic drinks.

The opportunity for his obstacle was to start a friendship club enterprise where he would not only meet new people, but also start a smart new business venture.

From this analysis the man ventured into an action plan aimed at understanding himself. He planned a way forward and implemented this personal plan of action in a committed way.

Discuss and evaluate the validity or sense of this example.

CASE STUDY: STORY OF AN ARTIST

In this story the focus is on the importance of maintaining a personal positive destiny.

It is said that an artist wanted to produce an artwork or portrait of Jesus and his disciples. It was relatively easy to find someone to pose as Jesus: He chose a good-looking, healthy young man. After that, various subjects came to pose as the disciples, with the exception of the last remaining figure. This person had to look like a dirty tramp. (Maybe the artist had someone like Judas, the traitor, in mind.)

After almost four years the artist eventually found someone who would suit the picture. He found this person in a park – a man with blood-shot eyes, a smelly individual who appeared to abuse alcohol and other substances, and who was dirty, like a tramp. Overjoyed, the artist invited this person to come and pose for him in his studio, in exchange for food.

As the man entered the studio, he turned around and astonished the artist by exclaiming:

"But Sir, I was here before! Then I posed as Jesus."

The life lesson from this story, is this: If you do not continuously work and manage your ideas in a positive way, negative thoughts can take over and direct your life into a mess. The problem is that negativity breeds further negativity. The person who had originally posed as Jesus was not in control nor was he the master of his own life, and therefore he eventually ended up as a real-life tramp and beggar.

Being the master of your own destiny starts with being in control of your own thoughts. Is it not amazing how the words you use, reflect what is going on in your mind?

If you keep your mind occupied with vulgar ideas, they surface in vulgar words which influence your habits, actions, values and eventually your destiny in life.

Therefore, the basic Ubuntu life lesson (origin unknown) demands the following:

> **Keep your thoughts positive, because they become your habits**
>
> **Keep your habits positive, because they become your actions**
>
> **Keep your actions positive because they become your values**
>
> **Keep your values positive, because they become your destiny**

To illustrate these processes, think of a glass filled with water.

Task: Sketch a glass which is half filled with water.

If the glass is only half full, the top half is a vacuum. If the glass represents your mind the water is the positive, and the vacuum the negative. For positive survival it is essential to fill the glass to its brim.

Task: Now sketch another glass which is filled to the brim with water.

Did you notice that when the glass is completely full, there is no vacuum or space for anything else?

In this very same way you continuously have to fill your mind with positive thoughts, thereby leaving no space for a vacuum, or for negative thoughts.

For discussion

What is the main lesson from the above story?
Which skill should you acquire to implement this life lesson?

The Ubuntu Counselling Process

INTRODUCTION

This chapter focuses on the analogy of the African pot. It will illustrate how to accommodate the overall counselling processes, and highlight the essential steps in this process. This will be followed by a general discussion on Ubuntu counselling.

ANALOGY OF "PITSENG" (AFRICAN POT)

When preparing food, it is traditional to cook maize in a three-legged, round, black pot over an open fire.

The cooking process consists of several steps, which are to be adhered to, to ensure the best end result – in this case some nice pap (porridge).

First of all, hard wood has to be gathered and stacked in a heap. Matches and kindling are needed to make the fire. Someone has to fetch water to pour into the pot. This is the **preparation process**.

Next some activities need to take place:

Someone has to light the fire. The pot must be placed over the fire and once the water is boiling, salt and maize must be added.

Hereafter the pot is covered with a lid, and the contents is left to cook and simmer. This is the **operational process**.

After some time has passed, the chef and his helpers remove the lid and dish out the contents (the cooked maize which has now become porridge) into a serving dish. From there the food is distributed onto plates. These actions make up the **self-management process**.

Now the porridge (the end result of the processes) may be enjoyed and supplemented with chakalaka (a tasty African sauce) or complemented with meat.

In the African environment a calabash filled with beer is circulated for all to enjoy (pouring some of the liquid onto the ground will also keep the ancestors happy, and assure them that they have not been forgotten).

In other cultures a bottle of wine is opened and poured into fine crystal glasses. This is called the **celebration or happiness process**.

The above processes may similarly be applied to Ubuntu counselling:

The preparation process includes all the actions necessary to initiate the broad counselling process. This includes collecting and studying material, finding a peaceful, warm environment which is conducive to counselling, adjusting to a questioning frame of mind, and all the technical or logistical requirements necessary for the counselling process. The preparation process is now called **input**.

The operational process is to assist the person or visitor in formulating the ideal, the dream, the end result, the vision. Dreams should meet the requirements of the acronym SMART – they should be specific, measurable, achievable, realistic and time-bound.

This process is followed by the mission statement of how this vision is to be realised, as well as a detailed and comprehensive ONPO analysis and a concrete programme of action. This is called the **counselling process**.

The management process contains all the activities flowing from the planning of the counselling process and the actual implementation of the programme. In addition, activities must be executed and regular after-care sessions and reviews (checks) have to be held. This is called **output**.

The final step in the process is the observation of manifestations of positive results of the greater philosophical counselling process, namely a customer's new-found direction, or being able to live a more meaningful life. A meaningful life is the end result of the counselling process (the final product (like the porridge) or vision made real). This is called the **outcome**.

"PITSENG"
(AFRICAN THREE-LEGGED POT) METHOLOGY

INPUT	PROCESS	OUTPUT	OUTCOME	CHECK
"Pitseng" pot				
Resources (fire, water, maize)	Cooking	Serving	Porridge	
Councelling				
Resources	Active listening Questioning ONPO	Action plan	Realised vision	

For Discussion: "Pitseng" Exercise

Find an actual pot.
Make a fire.
Prepare a meal.
Discuss the reality of input,
process,
output
outcome.

Counselling Through Ubuntu

The challenge to investigate and change your own life, or that of another person or persons in accordance with the above steps, is both exciting and practical.

Changing lifestyles is all about starting new ways of living.

People do not always value life in a positive manner. In some instances certain events cause people to act in a negative way or to be depressed.

The problem with a negative or depressed mindset is that it has an extremely strong in influence on others: In a life or work (team) situation it is a real killer which contributes to excessive and unhealthy stress. It is also a stumbling blocks for creative thinking. Negative thoughts should therefore be eliminated vigorously, the moment they appear in your mind or in any situation.

Miserable people influence situations negatively. They may not qualify for conventional psychological or psychiatric treatment, but on the other hand they should not be allowed to spread their negativity to others.

We have dealt with the basic values of Ubuntu, namely humanness, caring, sharing, respect and compassion. These very basic values can be used to counsel others and help them employ positive thinking in an Ubuntu sense. In other words, accepting these values may contribute to the formulation of someone's vision or mission, help them to work on an ONPO analysis, formulate an action programme or plan, and implement the steps of an own, personal action route.

THE ROLE
OF COUNSELLOR

The role of the counsellor or helper is to guide the other person to perform the above actions himself or herself, in a holistic sangoma way. This implies that the person or customer should truly trust the counsellor or helper to reveal all his or her hidden problems and pleasures.

Hidden problems come to the fore in the successful use of the brainstorming or heartstorming techniques.

Senghor (1965:15) points out that Africans are very emotive, while in the Western world the mind is everything (I think, therefore I am). Africans says it's all is in the heart (I feel, therefore I am).
In the Western world intelligence is measured according to rational criteria. In Africa, intelligence is emotional.

This is also a reference to what is called Socratic philosophical counselling, which is now being practised in countries like Germany, Holland, the United States, Israel and South Africa.

In Western philosophy, the roots of philosophical counselling go back to Socrates and Plato in ancient Greece. Another prominent counselling figure was Confucius Lao Tzu, of imperial China.

Counsellor-philosophers were greatly respected as life-coping advisors, whose counsel was sought on personal issues.

Like sagacity, philosophical counselling has been practised all over Africa for ages. African sages shared their wisdom orally, to the benefit of the community, by providing guidance to individuals faced with moral dilemmas.

Basically, philosophical counselling is a therapeutic method for a healthier life. (What is the meaning of life? Why am I alive? How best is life to be enjoyed and appreciated as a fun experience?)

This method is about the process of developing life-coping skills (tools for counselling), like relaxed concentration, attentive listening, Socratic questioning, and critical self-evaluation. The process leads to wisdom – you discover solutions to life problems and lay down personal guidelines for a healthy life.

Philosophical counselling is a relatively new field of philosophy. During philosophical counselling the skills of interpretation and perspective are used to help clients determine what their perspectives are, and to reduce anxiety and stress. It does not have to be a rigid, rational exercise.

The Socratic method is generally applied as a questioning process where an attitude of doubt prevails. Questioning requires a human response.

Philosophy, since Socrates, has been a study of humankind, of how one is supposed to live and why. Giving meaning to the burden of life and leading someone to different perspectives provide them with guidance in the art of living. By finding answers (to questions about the meaning of life, why one is alive, what the best life is) philosophical counselling becomes a therapeutic method for a healthier life. A healthier life is indicative of having found some direction, of greater independence and self-determination based on self-regulation.

A healthier life is one which has less stress – stress being characterised by symptoms like anxiety, aggression, constant irritability, a lack of concentration, the inability to socialise, the desire to abuse alcohol or drugs, and anti-social behaviour.

The Ubuntu counsellor does not enforce his own ideas but helps someone arrive at the birthing of new ideas which will give more meaning to his or her life. It is about clarifying and understanding the roots of personal hang-ups.

The meaning of words and concepts related to the seeker's dilemma must therefore be clarified by the person himself: The counsellor merely helps the person find meaning in life.

The person is not seen as a patient but is described as a visitor or seeker (because he is in search of self-knowledge) or even as a customer. This is to avoid labelling people as "sick".

In the Western world it is a well-known practice for people to be referred to medical doctors, psychologists, psychiatrists or ministers of religion to help them solve personal problems. Western medical doctors are trained to treat the symptoms of illnesses and diseases, and not the people themselves. Psychologists and psychiatrists help people with serious psychological hang-ups and issues by categorising them, and then treating them according to the specific psychological boxes in which they have been placed. It can be argued that psychologists' attempts to categorise people according to various psychological illnesses is unfair to the person, who should instead play some role in gaining self-understanding through a Socratic form of discourse – as philosopher-counsellors do.

Psychotherapists prefer to use "scientific" criteria of a certain school of thought when realigning the patient to a more normal or conventional state of mind.

Ministers of religion classify and judge people according to their sins. The methodology employed is the utilisation of prayers.

In New Zealand the Maori tradition of healing physical and emotional problems (stress-related problems) makes use of prayer.

In Ubuntu, the sangoma's way of counselling follows a more holistic and human approach. Sangomas and traditional healers tend to try to help the person as a whole, and do not treat a specific symptom in isolation. This African counselling process is also referred to by Wamba-dia-Wamba (Presbey, 1996:8) as "Nzonzi" where counsellors appear to be masters in the art of listening attentively and tirelessly, to pick up the essence of each word spoken, to observe every look, every gesture, every silence, in order to grasp their respective significance."

This leads to counter arguments and elaboration, which remind one of the Socratic arguments which were also based on attentive listening and intense questioning in order to find ethical and just solutions.

The counsellor should be empowered to direct the visitor to discover his or her own solutions to problems through the application of the ONPO analysis (as proposed in the previous section) which is based on self-understanding and healing. In other words, by applying this analysis people become more self-aware and self-analysis-oriented, arriving at answers to their questions by clarifying their own thoughts, actions and attitudes.

This could very well be compared to the role of an Ubuntu-oriented barman in a shebeen (African pub) listening to the day-to-day chat of his visitors: He does not advise or prescribe but lends a sympathetic ear to their problems and difficulties.

By creating a relaxed and harmonious atmosphere of trust he inspires his visitors to talk and review problems and to find solutions for themselves.

Most importantly, the counsellor always refrains from giving advice: His role is merely to question, listen actively and encourage the visitor to find his own solutions.

The characteristics of an Ubuntu counsellor are the following: He or she

➢ practises the skill of philosophising by analysing concepts (conceptual analysis), has the ability to investigate world views (the influence of culture), to apply critical thinking (questioning the validity of assumptions and perceptions), and facilitates an examination of the self (moving a person to self-analysis the Socratic way)

➢ creates a conducive counselling environment (cosy, friendly, relaxed)

➢ respects the dignity of the person, which is an outward expression of the inherent worth of a character

➢ wins the trust of the seeker or visitor

➢ is completely objective and not influenced by own cultural and social beliefs or values (setting aside own ideas and opinions)

➢ listens actively: If speech is the mirror of the soul, it stands to reason that as a man speaks, so he is

➢ has mastered and is able to practise the skills of caring, empathy, sympathy, respect, compassion

➢ is able to assist the seeker or visitor in developing a personal plan (as set out in the "Pitseng" process) in a very subtle manner, including the facilitation of the ONPO process

➢ persists with counselling assistance even in events of unpleasantness (the seeker becoming irritated or indulging in emotional outbursts)

➢ gains some perspective on the dilemma of that person.

Ubuntu Skills | 11

A WORD OF CAUTION

At the start of this book Ubuntu was defined as an ancient philosophy or world view with its roots anchored in traditional African mystic life.

It has a mystical, mostly unwritten, theoretical and physical origin and history which are embedded in Africa, and which were allegedly formed especially in the northern part of the continent.

It is widely believed that Africa was the cradle of all mankind and this assumption has awakened tremendous interest in the genesis of African wisdom and the structuring of African society.

Ubuntu history is both mystical and exciting. It also manifests in the thinking of others in the international world.

It is, for example, alleged (Broodryk: 2005, op cit:Introduction) that the legendary Sir Richard Branson, international entrepreneur, shocked the business world and conventional leaders by adopting a new human management philosophy and style based on a family-type business where happiness and even fun in the workplace are encouraged!

After all, to some work is merely work. To rigidly thinking autocrats, work is not about having fun. On the contrary, to them work is too serious a matter to make any allowances for pleasure: Pleasure is restricted to employees' private time.

Branson has therefore been practising Ubuntu even though he does not originate from Africa.

Regarding life-coping skills, the famous American expert on positive thinking, Dale Carnegie, in his famous work *How to win friends and influence people* (of which 21 million copies have been sold to date), identified several positive life lessons which can help human beings cope with the sorrows and problems of life.

These guidelines have also helped the author of this book personally throughout his life, to keep transforming life's negatives - the threats and blockages - into positive opportunities and solutions.

It is with a deep respect for Carnegie's positive thoughts and lessons that a comparison is made between Ubuntu life skills and this author's positive thinking guidelines.

Africans are known to be basically accommodating and forgiving, since all people are regarded as brothers and sisters of a greater brotherhood.

While comparing positive notions, these highly respected and to an extent sacred life-coping lessons will also culminate in the findings of the previous chapters. It is therefore advisable to study the foregoing chapters before reading the final chapter separately, in order to avoid misunderstanding and a possible crisis of perception.

The aforementioned findings, being related to the values of Ubuntu, will be directly linked to the basic beliefs of the ideal Ubuntu person. From integrated links between values and beliefs it will become clear what the great life-coping lessons entail.

THE UBUNTU PERSONALITY

The "Ubuntu personality" refers to the ideal human being as he or she embodies the ancient Ubuntu values.

The ideal man, who according to the Ubuntu world view possesses all these virtues of Ubuntu, can be described as

- a kind person
- generous
- living in harmony
- friendly
- modest
- helpful
- humble
- happy.

These virtues arose from the traditional African way of life, which was peaceful and harmonious. Respect was shown not only to other human beings, but also to the communal environment, animals, nature and the supernatural.

The well-known African poet and philosopher Leopold Senghor, who also was the leader of the Negritude intellectual movement in Africa, gave a much-respected description (Bhengu, op cit:16) of the African personality, which is similar to the Ubuntu personality.

According to Senghor African people have a certain way of living, speaking, singing, dancing, laughing, crying, painting and sculpting. Many Africans regard this way of life as unique and peculiar to Africa alone.

It is this reference to a certain way of life that makes Ubuntu so different from other cultures. Africans are generally hesitant to try and give a clear-cut definition of this unique type of partly (or on occasion totally) uninhibited expression of their appreciation for life, even in times of temporary misery.

It is difficult to define. It is a natural response flowing from a happy approach to life.

A happy approach to life is closely linked to positive thinking. Negative thinking is like a virus, an enemy which represents evil, disaster, misery, depression and unhappiness.

The Ubuntu personality therefore embodies the sum of the positive cultural values of Ubuntu and the African world.

The Ubuntu personality is very necessary in today's world where violence, exploitation, abuse and horrific material greed seem to dominate life patterns: The African personality is in direct opposition to these awful practices and trends. This personality is devoted to the pursuit of committed humanness.

Global Ubuntu living is, therefore, essential for all the inhabitants of this world.

The main African message is to rejoice in the flourishing humanness of the new century, which has already been labelled "the African century".

In order to understand the Ubuntu personality, which may be mystic or strange to especially Westerners and other cultures outside Africa, the beliefs of the ideal Ubuntu (wo)man or personality are to be nourished, as they contain the basic life-coping lessons and skills for a happy life - one of quality.

These beliefs or skills can apply to all cultures, and will be presented with an indication of the Carnegie and other Western value counterparts relevant to each respective Ubuntu guideline.

U<small>BUNTU</small> SKILLS

The following Ubuntu skills are to be mastered for a better life (the Senghor life wisdom is indicated in brackets under each skill heading):

THE SKILL OF TOGETHERNESS
(M<small>Y NEIGHBOUR AND</small> I <small>HAVE THE SAME ORIGINS, SAME LIFE EXPERIENCE AND A COMMON DESTINY</small>)

The emphasis is on sameness and "umoja" (togetherness). We are together in this life and as a cooperative and community we are heading for the same end result. Let us then be brothers in our brotherhood.

By being together we can share what we have, our thoughts included.

Carnegie advises people to encourage others to talk about themselves, and thus share experiences.

Africans have a habit of inspiring others to talk, in great detail, about where they hail from, how their family is, how life is treating him or her, etc. This is a comprehensive process.

The relevant skill is to establish a spirit of unity and commonality between people. If people share common experiences, it creates a feeling of togetherness.

THE SKILL OF BROTHERHOOD
(WE ARE THE OBVERSE AND REVERSE SIDES OF ONE ENTITY)

Ubuntu brotherhood is based on the expression that "I am a person through other persons".

If not for the comradeship (intense friendship) of others in the community, people would derive less enjoyment from life. The meaning of life is drawn from the social and physical inter-dependence of people.

People rely on each other for survival and support. As individuals, not all people are strong. If they stand together and rejoice in their collective co-existence, they are strong.

In Ghana an analogy is made (Oduro, op cit:3) as found in the saying that "a tree cannot survive a storm on its own".

In Zulu the relevant word is "simunye" (solidarity): It is easy to break a single twig, but if may twigs are bound into a bundle, they become impossible to snap.

A person should therefore involve others as brothers or team members for general support. When faced as a team, the problems of life seem lighter, since a variety of inputs and advice can be derived from the relevant experiences of others. In Africa the members of a group tend to work together as a collective, to solve individual problems.

Mbigi (1995:111) refers to the "Collective Fingers Theory". According to this the thumb, in order to work efficiently, will need the collective cooperation of the other fingers. In practice it means that one needs to open collective forums which are inclusive in nature, and must, as far as possible, include everyone in a group.

A spirit of brotherhood is also essential for successful teamwork.

Characteristics of effective brotherhood teams are identified (Harvard Business Essentials, 2004:96) as

➤ competence (everyone brings something the team needs)
➤ a clear and compelling goal
➤ commitment to the common goal
➤ every member contributes
➤ every member benefits
➤ a supportive environment is created
➤ alignment becomes possible.

One of the largest events companies in South Africa, eParty Design, accepted Ubuntu as its business philosophy.

All staff members receive training in Ubuntu, before being divided into tribes or strategic unit teams (SUTs) for purposes of cohesion (to create a family atmosphere). These Ubuntu SUTs now work, through continuous improvement, to embrace Ubuntu values and to incorporate the Ubuntu Code of Conduct and the Ubuntu Pledge in everything they do in the workplace.

All team members participate in practical workshops on the implementation of Ubuntu in their daily work situations.

Being brothers and sisters provides a "we"-feeling, which is conducive to cohesiveness (esprit de corps). The "we"-feeling encourages every member of a society, in any country, village and workplace, to completely identify with the rest of his or her society or community or extended family. It evokes a sense of belonging, security and certainty. The "we"-feeling creates camaraderie.

According to Koka (1996 b:10) a sense of belonging is evident in the spirit of oneness which people experience, as is evident in the saying "You touch one, you touch all".

THE SKILL OF EQUALITY
(WE ARE UNCHANGING EQUALS)

In Africa all people are equal. There is no categorisation on the basis of class.

If one person progresses materially and receives more than others, the surplus will be shared with the underprivileged brothers and sisters.

Africa does not allow some to eat while others go hungry, nor does it allow some to sleep warm while others are left out in the cold.

The idea of social class being based on wealth, is absurd as far as Africans are concerned.

Carnegie stresses the importance of making the other person feel important, and of the need to it sincerely, no matter who the person is. All people should be treated with dignity and respect.

The Constitution of South Africa, which is based on Ubuntu values, also demands that the human dignity of all people be respected and protected. This is precisely in line with the notion that all people are important and equal irrespective of income, gender, race and culture. Mankind is an integrated whole consisting of different material environments, sexes, race groups and cultures: All race and cultural groups are appreciated as being equal.

Since all people's customs are also respected, it is a good idea to give recognition to the importance of people's names. In the past, Westerners encouraged blacks to adopt colonial names because they did not know how to pronounce their African names, which had been given to them on the day of their birth. The African custom of giving babies descriptive, traditional names is not an inferior practice. It is a unique custom which has its justification in acknowledging that all persons are important. It also emphasises the joyous occasion of a child's birth, irrespective of whether that individual is born into wealth or poverty.

Babies are given names with a very relevant meaning, and that name has special meaning to that child.

Practising the life-coping skill of treating all people as equals will, in return, result in goodwill and engender friendly attitudes from others.

THE SKILL OF SHARING
(WE ARE MUTUALLY FULFILLING COMPLEMENTS)

Sharing is an important African value.

People have different qualities, talents and resources which should be shared in a spirit of cooperativeness to ensure positive living. Everyone should cooperate as sharing human beings and people should aim to complement one another. This is indicative of someone living according to the values of open-handedness and supportiveness, in accordance with their needs and the needs of others.

Needs - be they physical or spiritual - are established when the discussion focuses on what would be in the best interest of the other person.

Carnegie refers to the use of dialogue as a tool. The challenge is to speak in terms of the other person's interests, thereby determining how one can strengthen him or her in life challenges.

The life-coping skill is to provide complementary capacity-building assistance to others.

THE SKILL OF SYMPATHY
(MY NEIGHBOUR'S SORROW IS MY SORROW)

Sympathy is vital in Ubuntu life, and is mainly practised in times of sorrow. Sorrow is an obstacle in life and it is inevitable that sorrow will appear from time to time in the form of death, illness or other hurtful events. When sorrow strikes a neighbour who is also a brother, a person experiences that sorrow too and weeps with that brother, because it is due to such a brother that a person is a brother to others too. But there is the realisation that that sorrow is temporary in nature.

Carnegie teaches man to accept the inevitable. Sorrow is also inevitable.

One core component of dealing with the sorrow of others (according to Frost, 2003:63) is to listen with compassion to someone else's pain. Just being emotionally present for someone who is hurting can help them feel they have been heard and that their feelings have been validated. This kind of emotional listening can help heal the wound.

This skill is also known as emotional intelligence. It is about being aware of someone else's emotional condition (as well as your own) and includes the ability to manage both. A person who attempts to help may also, to an extent, absorb the emotions experienced by someone else.

However, there are some incidents or situations which cannot be resolved at all. Nothing, for instance, is as certain as death. We find consolation for this statement in the concept that God gave man

➢ the serenity to accept the things he cannot change

➢ the courage to change the things he can and

➢ the wisdom to know the difference between the two.

This notion is universally positive, and is also applicable to the Ubuntu world view. It is a useful tool in the counselling process where people are living with serious terminal illness, or a disease like HIV/AIDS, as well as mental or physical disability. These are usually situations no one can cure: You have to accept the inevitable, since it falls outside the power and capabilities of man to change things.

You can, however, relatively easily change other situations, for example by quitting smoking or drinking (both moderately and excessively), or getting rid of excess weight, or by not indulging in self-pity and depressive moods.

The life-coping skill is to practise sincere sympathy in your relations with others: A sorrow shared, is a sorrow halved.

THE SKILL OF HAPPINESS
(MY NEIGHBOUR'S JOY IS MY JOY)

A joy shared, is a joy doubled. Double joy is happiness.

Life is about experiencing the greatest true form of happiness at all times. That is also called qualitative happiness. This form of happiness can be obtained through the creation of a spontaneous brotherhood of man.

Standing together, enjoying and celebrating together, creates a spirit of cohesiveness. This manifests as togetherness, warmth and cheerfulness.

The pursuit of happiness is claimed (Parrot, 1987:13) to be among the inalienable rights of any human being, and two ideas are pin-pointed as being important to anyone who wishes to live out their happiness with inward joy.

Firstly, happiness is a process, a pursuit and a way of life. Happiness is a habit - when practised constantly is so powerful that it can dominate any of a person's other attitudes.

Secondly, others will interfere with your happiness if you let them. However, if your right to be happy is controlled from within, you remain in charge of your own happiness.

In order to live a happy life, Carnegie suggests that you crowd worry out of your mind by keeping busy. Alternatively, you should try to get involved in an activity that requires all your attention. In this way, there will be no opportunity for your mind to dwell on worries. Worry and stress are universal, negative conditions of the mind. Traditionally, Africans do not experience these all that often: Life is there to enjoy, not to worry about.

Worrying about issues should be filed appropriately in the diary of mind. For example, if any issue is to be addressed on Friday, you should diarise or leave the issue and only attend to it on Friday. In that way, the preceding days will not spoil your worry-free existence.

On Friday, follow these steps to address the problem:

➤ Define the exact problem

➤ Identify the specific root of the problem

➤ Develop solutions to the problem

➤ Prioritise these solutions and decide on the best one

➤ Identify two alternative solutions if the best solution is not suitable

➤ Implement the best solution.

These steps are complementary to the main aim of this book, namely to suggest the active living and implementation of more worry-free, and less stressful Ubuntu life-coping skills.

Keeping busy, as Carnegie suggested, also implies more informal discussion, and greater concentration through active listening to the opinions and deliberations of others. In practising these habits, there is limited time for worry and fear.

Fear is evil. Religious faiths condemn fear. It is stated 365 times in the Bible (equalling the total number of days in the year) that man must not fear or be afraid. If you fear or worry, too little space is left in the mind to accommodate happy and creative thinking.

To live a happy life, other human beings should be complemented on achievements, and receive sincere gratitude for favours done. Carnegie proposes that one show honest and sincere appreciation to others. This advice also applies to Ubuntu. Being recognised and acknowledged is one of the strongest positive tools in inculcating self-respect in the soul of a fellow human being. Ubuntu builds the self-esteem of people by being caring and appreciative in its very nature: Man is a human being through other human beings, and if another person is appreciated in a sincere way, the one who shows appreciation is also appreciating himself in the process.

Expressions of appreciation should be genuine, and not be given to win someone else's favour: This says much about someone's credibility.

It is stated (Kouzes et al, in Jossey-Bass, 2005:21) that a leader (remember all people are leaders in some way) should lead the way, inspire a shared vision, challenge the process, enable others to act, and encourage the heart. It is this encouragement of the heart that is the secret to motivating others. People tend to be more loyal to a leader or person (even in the workplace) if well-meant and honest recognition is given. Research indicates that the main requirement followers have for following someone willingly, is honesty. Honesty is usually linked to virtues such as truthfulness, ethical behaviour and principled guidance, and it emerges as the single most important ingredient in the leader-constituent relationship.

This finding is not surprising: People have the right to demand moral regeneration and the maintenance of positive values like the ones advocated by an Ubuntu lifestyle.

It is a well-known practise in Africa for kings to be shown sincere appreciation by joyous praise singers. According to Mutwa (1997:18) the praise singer was a professional artist in traditional society and the most important person in African culture. His duty was to recount both the positive and negative deeds of the sovereign in an honest way. Details of the king's bad temper, for example, or his latest misdemeanour would be included. All the battles the king had engaged in - his victories and defeats - were faithfully recounted in elaborate and ceremonial language. The praise songs had to reflect a true and correct appreciation for the king's past deeds.

Motivation happens when others are recognised for good work or deeds. According to Carnegie the secret lies in arousing in the other person an eagerness to perform. Carnegie tries to encourage people to influence others to become enthusiastic about a positive idea or venture.

Ubuntu people are by nature happy and enthusiastic, and this friendly spirit is evident in their daily life. Laughter and socialising occur informally, and are usually enjoyed with natural and spontaneous passion.

THE SKILL OF EMPATHY
(HE AND I ARE MUTUALLY FULFILLED WHEN WE STAND BY EACH OTHER IN MOMENTS OF NEED)

Empathy is the ability to put yourself in someone else's place or situation. The person who can master empathy successfully will also experience satisfaction from helping to meet the needs of others, since it is through empathy that one realises what the need of others are.

If you walk a mile in someone else's shoes, it may be shocking to realise what a strain it is for that person to be with you (you may be selfish, greedy or uncooperative).

Carnegie encourages people to talk about themselves, and not to talk in their own selfish interest. This is not a unique way of thinking. Africans encourage others to talk about themselves when enquiring in great detail about where the other person hails from, how his family is, etc.

Carnegie stresses the importance of being an active listener.

It is argued (Sample in Jossey-Bass, op cit:356) that most people, including many leaders, are terrible listeners; they actually think talking is more important than listening. Modern, open-minded leaders know it is better to listen first and talk later. And when they listen, they do so artfully. Artful listening is an excellent means of acquiring new ideas and gathering and assessing information. It is absolutely essential in any counselling process.

If you can listen attentively without being quick to judge, you will often get a fresh perspective that will help you think independently. The art of listening can help you understand the thinking of others.

The attributes of effective listeners are identified (Lucas, 1994:57) as: Being alert, interested, responsive, attentive, not being distracted, being understanding, caring and cautious, not interrupting, being empathetic, patient, other-centred and an effective evaluator. Ineffective listeners are apathetic, inattentive, defensive, disinterested, impatient and distracted.

Active listening is an important feature of African conversation. Sangomas (African psychologists) are known to have mastered the art of active listening in their daily counselling of patients.

It is generally also a feature of Ubuntu people to listen actively to the problems and words of others. The way in which words are expressed is also indicative of a person's mood.

Mandela (op cit:68) remembers that he encouraged cabinet members in Parliament to air their divergent views in great detail. He encouraged people to listen carefully, then make a summary of the views which would eventually result in good resolutions which everyone could agree to (a form of consensus). In doing so, all had ownership in decisions, which in turn create greater commitment.

Sindane (1994:4) refers to this form of consensus as an example of how Africans view democracy.

Democracy is described as "sitting under a tree and talking until everybody (more or less) agrees".

The African system of democracy or consensus is about giving all a chance to express views and for all to listen and discuss standpoints, until everybody reached agreement.

THE SKILL OF COMPASSION
(HIS SURVIVAL IS A PRECONDITION FOR MY SURVIVAL)

In order to survive in a world of natural disasters, poverty and unforeseen events, mankind is dependent on the survival of all.

This interdependence of human beings creates an interpersonal bond of care and love. In Africa people show their care and love for human beings in very explicit ways. Public leaders and even ordinary people often hug each other while greeting heartily, and long enquiries may follow about the circumstances of the other person, his family, extended family, etc. This is in sharp contrast to some other cultures where a cold and formal way of greeting is the convention.

In Africa human care is recognised in expressions of compassion.

Carnegie promotes compassion by advising people to become genuinely interested in others.

Ubuntu is basically about humanness and its focus is also on becoming interested in the fate of human beings. The relevant Ubuntu prescriptive is to care for (and thus be interested in) one's sisters and brothers within the human family, which correlates closely with Carnegie's advice.

From the Ubuntu perspective it is not acceptable for some people to eat heartily while others go hungry: To be genuinely interested in other people is to care for all. In this respect, Ramose (op cit:150) refers to the saying "motho ke motho ka botho" (the essence of caring for others).

In Ubuntu culture and African morality man, in order to enjoy the status of being human, must comply with the rules of "Botho" (Ubuntu). One example is that it is contrary to Ubuntu to refrain from sharing whatever one has, with those in need. Ubuntu people who are employed continue to share their wages and salaries by way of caring for their unemployed kith and kin.

THE SKILL OF RESPECT
(NO COMMUNITY HAS ANY RIGHT TO DETERMINE THE DESTINY OF OTHER COMMUNITIES OR ANY OTHER PERSON)

Respect for other persons - their spiritual, religious, political, economic and cultural beliefs and customs - is of cardinal importance in all encounters in life.

Never should other people or communities be prescribed to, or forced away from their own conventions.

Africa has along history of colonial oppression by Western countries, which included Westerners enforcing certain prescriptions on communities or persons, thereby changing their destinies. Africans were confronted with an acceptance of Western political, religious and economic dogmas which were in sharp contrast to the beliefs of Africa itself.

In the political arena democracy (the Western way) was enforced, ignoring the way Africans had practised their own traditional consensus model of democracy (government of national unity) for ages.

As regards religion, it was noted that traditional religious beliefs and mediators were made a laughing stock by Western missionaries who did not appreciate the seriousness of African beliefs when it came to the continued existence of the ancestors. In the spiritual world three types of ancestors were identified (Mbigi, 1997:53): Positive ancestral spirits, positive oracular nature spirits (as found in animals and places (like in pools and trees)), and evil spirits.

As regards economics, Westerners succeeded in making the perception of capitalism extremely unattractive to Africans. This was especially the case where capitalism benefited a few privileged white owners of huge enterprises financially, at the cost of exploiting underprivileged African workers.

This prescription is also not new when applied to African thinking.

Traditionally, extended families helped each other plough lands. The challenge was to finish the job before the rains came. Once they had met the challenge, social celebrations ("pungwe") were held.

THE SKILL OF TOLERANCE
(MY NEIGHBOUR IS ME IN A DIFFERENT GUISE)

People have a tendency to judge and belittle others who adhere to strange or unfamiliar customs or patterns of behaviour.

The point is that people should show greater tolerance towards different religions, beliefs and cultures.

African people are not easily rushed merely for the purpose of being punctual. Westerners have a reputation for being governed by time and live out the belief that time is money. Time is not money. Holding very productive, long discussions may - in the long term - generate more money than quick, formal and impersonal deliberations do.

Long discussions are also linked to the concept of African time, as is the tendency of not adhering strictly to meeting times. Africans, as regards time consciousness, exercise tolerance.

Tolerance is promoted if people have a say in ideas and decisions. Carnegie advises that the other person should feel that the idea is his or hers.

This is also very Ubuntu-like. In the Ubuntu workplace everybody is part of the collective extended family style of business. Meetings are held as a team (they are attended by all, not merely by a few managers) and as a collective all ideas are shared. Once resolutions have been passed, everyone has the privilege of thinking that the resolution was also his idea.

This is one reason why all opinions are valuable. Mandela refers (op cit) to African etiquette which dictates that a person should be allowed to state his case without any interruption whatsoever - as should the other party. In this way all opinions receive a fair hearing and due consideration.

This means that everyone is bound to implement the collective decision of the team, because all have ownership of the resolution.

The emphasis is, however, not on the individual: It is not "I" who scored, but "we" who decided - the individual is merely part of the "we".

THE SKILL OF LOVE
(EQUALS DO NOT OPPRESS EACH OTHER)

In Africa oppression is not a popular concept, and no group or culture is superior to another.

Oppressive attitudes are rejected by the masses and within the family, oppression is not tolerated at all.

In Setswana folktales a prominent story which is told (Malimabe, 1999:3) to children, under the name "Segwagwe le Leswafe", deals with a couple who for many years struggled to have children.

Eventually they were blessed with two children: One was a frog and the other an albino. The albino had sores all over her body, and because of her unfortunate appearance, she was left in a bush to die. The frog baby was very lazy and did not do the chores she was supposed to do during the day. She rather spent the day visiting her friend, the hippopotamus. During her absence, the albino baby would come out, clean the house and cook delicious food. The frog ate and relaxed, thinking that the chores had been done by magic. The oblivious parents were very happy with the state of affairs.

One day the father decided to remain home to watch the frog baby doing her chores. He was surprised to see the albino baby sneaking into the home, and doing everything. When the albino baby tried to return to the thorn bush, the father grabbed her and held her so tightly she could not escape. The albino was welcomed back by the parents.

The lesson is that one should never discriminate against another on the basis of appearance, disability or race.

The life-coping skill of love is highly honoured in African family and community life, and emotive feelings can manifest in various positive ways - both physically, and through body language. All people are treated as equals.

Certain respectful conventions and rituals may, however, be mistaken for signs of superiority. One example is the convention of not looking dignitaries (like chiefs) directly in the eye. This gesture, however, is a sign of respect. Chiefs and people in leadership positions are known to be democratic and supportive. Everybody is granted an equal opportunity to state their case or opinion.

Carnegie comments that respect should be shown for the other person's opinions, and one should never directly say: "You are wrong". One should rather try to understand the reason for another person's opinions or actions.

Respecting the opinions of others is part and parcel of Ubuntu culture.

In traditional Africa the king had advisors (indunas) and when they were having meetings about problems within the community (their kraal), all elders were invited to participate in the deliberations. Everyone was entitled to his opinion and nobody was regarded as being wrong or right. They would deliberate endlessly until they reached consensus, which was eventually accepted by all as the correct ruling or outcome.

Carnegie further advises that if you are wrong, you should admit it quickly and emphatically. Being able to admit to mistakes and to apologise, is not an unknown phenomenon in Africa. This is a matter of honesty, and the Ubuntu Pledge demands that people live honestly and positively.

All political parties and religious groups in South Africa support the Ubuntu Pledge. As noted previously, the Pledge prescribes that people be good and do well, that they live honestly and positively, be considerate and kind, care for brothers and sisters in the human family, respect the rights of others to their own beliefs and cultures, care for and improve the environment, promote peace, harmony and non-violence, and that they promote the welfare of the country as patriotic citizens.

In respect of honesty, Ubuntu also does not differ fundamentally from the Carnegie guidelines.

THE SKILL OF HUMANNESS
(TO BE INHUMANE IS TO BE SUB-HUMAN)

The biggest lesson Africa can export to the world is how to appreciate the value of being non-barbaric - in other words, to practise humanness. Humanness is also the very essence of Ubuntu. It is due to this affinity with humanness that apartheid South Africa never experienced a bloody revolution. This is the humanness which saw a convicted but very dignified Nelson Mandela leave prison after 27 years as a political prisoner - not as an embittered person, but as a statesman propagating understanding and reconciliation between all races in South Africa.

One human gesture in Carnegie tradition is to start conversations in a friendly manner. Here Carnegie touches on an important aspect of Ubuntu communication behaviour. In Africa it is good manners to greet others heartily and enthusiastically, and to enquire in-depth about the other person's well-being, before discussing any other issues.

This sociable method of establishing instant interpersonal communication is not always evident in especially Western environments. Many Westerners tend to be quite satisfied with a mere cold greeting, like saying "Hi" to the other person without making further enquiries about his or her well-being.

Carnegie also recommends the use of a genuine, warm smile, which is good therapy when suffering from illness or depression.

Smiling is very important in African life, and is not peculiar to other cultures. Smiling and laughing are very basic behavioural elements of the daily Ubuntu lifestyle. This is the reason why cold and grim faces (as found in some other cultures) are strange to Ubuntu people.

The advantage of a smile is that it has a reflective response: Smile at strangers and they will usually smile in return. A smile breaks cold atmospheres and stressful situations.

A former ANC leader (Sisulu, op cit:1) told the author during an interview that he had felt more lonely in a certain part of Europe, which he visited after his release, than he had ever felt during his years in prison on Robben Island. On the island he had experienced the warmest compassion imaginable. All prisoners were comrades and close friends - they even shared toothbrushes. In Europe he found the people extremely cold and in a way even hostile towards one another.

The first social rule when meeting an African (for the purpose of communication) is to smile very broadly and naturally, and not to grin like a crocodile.

THE SKILL OF HARMONY
(ALL THAT ONE LIVES FOR IS TO BE THE BEST YOU CAN BE)

This piece of wisdom touches on the meaning of life and being at peace with yourself. It encourages people to endeavour to excel at whatever they do, and not to stress about irrelevant issues.

It does not matter whether you are a shepherd, academic, businessman, labourer, or chief - you only have to do your best, as an equal to all other human beings.

Not all people are intellectuals, leaders or businessmen. This does not mean that some are more equal than others, but merely that people have different roles to play. Being the best you can be, implies that you have to live life in peace and harmony.

Life has its ups and downs, but it is the harmonious person who finds solutions to everyday problems. Each person's best will depend on his or her talent and blessings. But if everybody strives to be a better person according to the values of Ubuntu, a new world order is bound to take shape - one that works for the benefit of all.

In this respect Carnegie warns that people should never criticise, condemn or complain, but should keep their cool. People tend to be easily overwhelmed, which leads to intolerance and stress-related behaviour under certain conditions.

The consequences of stress are devastating: Stress is said (Losyk, 2005:xvii) to be the single biggest reason why people (in modern societies) get sick or die prematurely: Every health problem - from headaches to heart attacks, psychosomatic disorders to strokes - can be linked to what is known as the plague of the twenty-first century.

The emotional impact of stress includes (ibid:15) negative behaviour, worry, obsessive thoughts, fear/phobia, sadness, irritability, anger/

rage, loneliness, confusion, hopelessness, insomnia, nightmares, depression and suicide.

These manifestations are totally against the spirit of Ubuntu. For example, traditionally suicide was completely unknown in African society. The tendency of children to commit suicide because they failed school subjects, is unheard of in African society. If a child fails a year at school, he or she merely returns to school the following year to repeat the course without feeling inferior or ashamed.

Having a harmonious personality can counteract stress, which mainly prospers in times of crisis.
During these periods it seems to be a natural tendency for people to criticise or condemn others, or to complain.

This type of behaviour does not promote harmonious relationships and disrupts the harmonious being of a person.

The skill of establishing harmony, which is to be exercised during these circumstances, comprises the ability to recognise an impending crisis, to maintain absolute calmness of mind, and not to allow emotions of anger and frustration to govern your behaviour.

Possible suggestions (Harvard, 2004a:63), which are applicable to all situations when it comes to recognising a crisis, are to pay attention when your instincts tell you something is wrong, to confront disturbing factors as you find them, to seek the counsel of others, and to let your values guide you.

Universal key principles (McKenna et al, in Jossey-Bass, op cit:564) in times of crises are to calmly attempt to get the facts, to identify the problem and decide how the situation should be handled, to involve others (delegate) if necessary, and to remember that in a crisis everything (even emotions or results) is magnified.

Crises should therefore be approached in a harmonious mode, as far as possible. Ubuntu is a philosophy that embraces harmonious thinking, talking and behaviour. Harmonious talking eases tensions in all situations. Mandela (op cit:172) says he discovered that in discussions it never helps to take a morally superior tone to another person or opponent: Superior tones and attitudes heighten tension. Kindness should prevail.

The skill of kindness is simple to practise: It manifests as helping crippled people across a busy street, holding open the door for someone, allowing another driver right of way on a highway, standing up in a crowded bus so that an elderly person can take a seat, giving beggars something to eat or drink, etc.

When it comes to practising more harmonious approaches, Ubuntu does not differ from the stated Carnegie prescription.

Ubuntu is indeed in essence about being applying non-critical attitudes to bring about more harmonious living. Even when others harm you, a cool approach should be followed. Keeping your cool is related to anger management. Anger management concerns people who are more "threat conscious" than others. Their personality and genetic make-up, as well as learned experiences throughout their lives, make them more likely to become angry without much provocation.

The appropriate solution to cool your anger, is to become aware of your rights, which include

- ➤ the right to an opinion
- ➤ the right to say 'no'
- ➤ the right to ask for what you want
- ➤ the right to make mistakes
- ➤ the right to put yourself first at times
- ➤ the right to change your mind
- ➤ the right to protest against unfair treatment or criticism.

These rights also apply to Ubuntu coping skills, with special emphasis on living in peace and harmony.

As Battion (2004:114) advises: "It has been said that the best revenge on people who have given you negative or witch messages, or wish you ill... is to live well - to live your life as if it were the only one you have, to make each moment count, to succeed at whatever has meaning for you. In a sense we are all dying from the moment of our birth: Some of us only take longer than others. Live well."

THE SKILL OF REDISTRIBUTION
(WEALTH MUST BE SHARED AND YOUR NEIGHBOUR'S POVERTY IS YOUR POVERTY)

The Ubuntu personality is focused on sharing, and does not accommodate the qualities of greed and selfishness.

The pursuit of individual wealth and riches is absent from traditional African life. This statement is supported by Hountondji (Sapina, 1997:15) who refers to "false Bantu" (meaning Africans with a lust for money): "I heard some older wise men repeating... these are men of lupeto and of money. They explained to me that these young people living with white men knew nothing about money, that was the only thing with any value of their life; they abandoned the wise Bantu vitality and respect for life for a philosophy of money; money is their only ideal; money is their goal; the supreme goal of their acts."

Asked about a definition of happiness, a Kenyan sage commented (Odera Oruka, 1991:99) as follows: "In our society, a happy man is he who has wealth and is ready to share it with others. Such a man is held in high esteem. So, for one to attain happiness, he should not just be a wealthy man, he should be a man who loves others too. Even a poor man can be happy, provided he mixes with others and shares whatever little he has with them."

The redistribution of wealth is a known convention in certain cultures and religions. Wealth does not include material assets only. It can also refer to non-material resources like knowledge and morality. It is recommended that those who have knowledge, share it with the have-nots.

The same applies to morality: If values of morality are unknown to an individual or group, it is only fair to educate them on the moral expectations of society.

Due to the high prevalence of HIV/AIDS in Africa, many orphans from affected families who cannot be accommodated by extended families, become street children and are much more likely to live without morals since there is no family educator to teach them social norms and values.
It is therefore necessary for informed persons to redistribute their knowledge on social morality to these orphans.

It is advisable to understand the needs of others, before you can share what assets you have. Carnegie emphasises that you should - in all honestly - try to see things from the other person's point of view. The Ubuntu viewpoint shares an understanding as regards this aspect of empathy and redistribution.

In Africa there are many different cultures. South Africa has eleven official languages. Amazingly, this fact does not give rise to any real conflict, because Africans use English as the medium of communication with other cultures, thereby putting themselves in the shoes of other groups and tribes on a daily basis. This helps them understand the opinions and viewpoints of others.

For example, an African delegate at a conference confessed to regularly reading Afrikaans newspapers to see "what make them tick" ("them" referring to white Afrikaners). In so doing, he makes an effort to put himself in the shoes of the other culture.

THE SKILL OF OBEDIENCE
(YOUR FATHER AND MOTHER'S LAWS ARE YOUR LAWS, YOUR RELATIVES' AND SOCIETIES' LAWS ARE MY LAWS)

Mores and customs are learnt within the family and extended family. This family atmosphere of Ubuntu is regarded (Ramose, op cit:102) as the basis for African law.

African law is about recognising the rights of groups. The group precedes and supersedes the individual.

Ubuntu customs and conventions, as the underlying components of African law, were transferred verbally throughout generations, to maintain order in African societies. Laws, ordinances, regulations and rules have as their sole purpose the structuring of society. They have to be obeyed to ensure order. Obeying the law of the family and society proves your obedience to the values of your cultural environment. These values are respected, and historically even manifested in names and nicknames people were given - all of them indicating some form of adherence to the law: "Obedience", "Order", "Respect", "Commitment" and "Trust" are just some such names.

Carnegie issues a reminder that a person's own name is the sweetest and most important sound in any language.

In the African environment traditional names have a special (respectful) meaning relating to an event which took place, or to a specific idea which was applicable at the moment of the baby's birth. If it was raining at that time, the baby might be named "Phumula" (soft rain). Another example is the name "Gatsha" (the name of a Zulu political leader) which means "branch of a tree". The idea is that he is like a branch, but will grow to become an entire tree himself as he progresses in life.

Sometimes a name also describes a person's character. An example hereof is the Zulu name "Nokulunga", which means "mother of kindness".

Respecting all people leads to obedience to interrelated conventions like being courteous. People in respectful cultures obey basic, positive conventions like adhering to dignified behaviour, exercising fairness in their relations with others and finding richness in other people.

In family and community life positive conventions pave the way for the development of ground rules. In this manner discipline is established to provide space for constructive co-existence between members of a tribe, community and nation.

Constructive co-existence is a reflection of the possibility of effective team or community work. It is alleged (Stone, 2003:170) that a sense of teamwork fosters greater commitment and builds momentum that leads to benefits like better problem solving, greater productivity, deriving greater joy from work or association, and a sense of purpose that is both motivating and fulfilling.

THE SKILL OF WISDOM
(KNOWLEDGE IS THE CHALLENGE OF BEING HUMAN SO AS TO DISCOVER THE PROMISE OF BEING HUMAN)

The African personality embraces humanism and the art of being a human person. Embracing humanism and humanness is an indication that such a person has gained vast knowledge on the subject. Gaining human knowledge is primarily to learn about Ubuntu and African humanism, which translates into wisdom.

These beliefs and guidelines are meant to make your own life - and the lives of those around you - more meaningful. They are typically African, and from the Ubuntu perspective they provide guidelines for the youth - in fact, for all generations - to honour, value and live according to.

The most important lesson of Ubuntu is for mankind to accept, strive towards and live according to the abovementioned basic, simple human values and principles for the attainment of the greatest individual and communal happiness.

In Africa life lessons and life-coping advice are given by sages. The Kenyan philosopher H. Odera Oruka recorded the wisdom of various sages, which merits closer study. The sages, when asked to explain their special roles in society and life in general, reported that their lives were devoted to the betterment of their communities, and the individuals within their communities.

Philosophy is about the love of wisdom. To be wise, is to possess the skill "to make mature judgements about the use of human knowledge in the context of daily life" (Presbey, 1997:3).

In every society one finds wise sayings. African sayings, which are often based on the experience of observing animals and natural phenomena, include (Leslau, 1985:15) the following:

IT IS A BAD CHILD WHO DOES NOT TAKE ADVICE

EVEN THOUGH THE OLD MAN IS STRONG AND HEALTHY, HE WILL NOT LIVE FOREVER

HE WHO CANNOT DANCE WILL SAY: THE DRUM IS BAD

TWO SMALL ANTELOPES CAN BEAT A BIG ONE

WHEN THE MOON IS NOT FULL, THE STARS SHINE MORE BRIGHTLY

LOVE IS LIKE A BABY: IT NEEDS TO BE TREATED TENDERLY

THE FROG WANTED TO BE AS BIG AS THE ELEPHANT, AND BURST

WHEN SPIDER NETS UNITE, THEY CAN TIE UP A LION

BECAUSE A MAN HAS INJURED YOUR GOAT, YOU DO NOT GO OUT
AND KILL HIS BULL

A LITTLE RAIN EACH DAY WILL FILL THE RIVERS TO OVERFLOWING

CROSS THE RIVER IN A CROWD AND THE CROCODILES WON'T EAT
YOU

HOWEVER FULL THE HOUSE, THE HEN FINDS A CORNER TO LAY IN

KNOWLEDGE IS LIKE A GARDEN: IF IT IS NOT CULTIVATED, IT
CANNOT BE HARVESTED.

These are typical wise sayings. However, this does not imply that all sayings found in Africa are wise. In this regard, Odera Oruka (1991:53) distinguishes between popular wisdoms or wise statements, commonplace statements, and foolish statements. Wisdom is expressed by the first category, while the second and third categories constitute the vast area of non-wisdom.

UBUNTU: PHILOSOPHY OF HAPPINESS

Ubuntu is - in essence - about happiness in true African style.

This happiness is spiritual, mental, and physical. Spiritual happiness is about abstaining from earthly wrongdoings and the elimination of obstacles affecting peaceful and meaningful life. Activities which hinder spiritual life are, for example, the social milieu people find themselves in - where there may be an obsession with material gain and greed, where people are exploited, where the pursuit of self-interest is a goal, and where physical, emotional and institutional violence are used.

Happiness in a spiritual sense is to be found in the pursuit of abstract beliefs, i.e. the non-visible and non-provable. It is about serious and intense faith. In Africa there is a belief in the existence of a Supreme Being who is approachable through the ancestors, who serve as mediators between the Being and the brotherhood of man.

If one simplifies religion, it could in the same way be argued that Christians are very similar in the way in which they believe in God, and that Muslims and Buddhists arrive at God in more or a less a related way.

From beliefs values are derived, which give meaning to life. For the African these are the Ubuntu and related values such as love, compassion, kindness, generosity, peace and harmony.

These values are applicable to all beliefs and cultures, but are not practised by all people. Imagine what a better world we can create if all people, irrespective of how they arrive at God or a super being, can practically manifest these communal values in their daily actions. By doing that, each person can make a small contribution to the Ubuntu ideal of godly living.

Godly living is spiritual.

Another prerequisite is a happy state of mind, where the power of thought is cardinal. Happiness is embedded in the brilliance of being a free thinker: You can actually choose which thoughts you prefer to entertain. A happy person's behaviour reflects a happy mind. Happiness is the prerequisite for enjoying qualitative life to the full. Qualitative and meaningful living manifest on a spiritual, mental and physical level.

It is holistic and all-encompassing, embracing the simple art of enjoying and appreciating life even in dark moments of illness, pain and distress - in fact, whenever you encounter life's negative obstacles.

African intellectuals refer to the Holy Belief of Maat as the basic foundation of Ubuntu, and its values are similar to those discussed in this chapter.

The main exponent of happiness in Western philosophy was Aristotle (384-322 B.C). For Aristotle (Presbey et al. 1995:445) the supreme good was *eudaimonia*, which is usually translated from the Greek as "well-being" or "happiness". Happiness is understood by Aristotle as the exercise of our natural faculties or talents in a manner which is virtuous. To act virtuously is to be happy, and happiness is a sign of virtuous action. Aristotle understands virtue as consisting of two varieties - intellectual and moral. Virtue itself is seen as a skill which is appropriate to each of our natural human faculties. Consequently, the skilful fulfilment of our human potential becomes the key to life.

This is similar to the Ubuntu skill of being the best you can be. That implies that you have to be the best that your specific faculties will allow.

Rogers (op cit:90) comes to the conclusion that people should trust and value the process that is themselves. For example, Einstein seems to have been unusually oblivious to the fact that good physicists did not appreciate his way of thinking. Rather than drawing back because of his inadequate academic preparation in Physics, he simply moved toward being Einstein, toward thinking his own thoughts, toward being as truly and deeply himself as he could be – with amazing results.

The ideal is to be at peace with all and everything. The solution is to acquire the ability to transform the negative into the positive, and to let go of everything you cannot control.

Remember that you only have one life.

The world has survived various natural disasters like tsunamis and hurricanes. In general it is widely believed that an asteroid will hit planet Earth, with disastrous consequences. Practically speaking, all life will come to an end. If this happens, destruction is inevitable. We must accept the inevitable, of which death is one example. Everybody has to die: It is an inevitability. Nothing is as certain as death.

On a positive note, the fact that we know about the inevitability of an asteroid hitting Earth has prompted scientists to start planning to employ nuclear methods to drive the oncoming asteroid off its course, to prevent such a tragedy. This will, however, just temporarily postpone our demise, and in the interim we will have to consider ways and means of making this life better and more meaningful.

In African thinking you become part of the ancestral world after your earthly life, meaning there is no heaven or hell in the afterlife. Members of other religious sects and faiths do not necessarily have to appreciate this belief, but the consolation is that in all religions, whatever happens after this earthly life seems to be for the better anyway.

CASE STUDY:
SURVIVING AN EARTHQUAKE

The following are extracts from an article (The Mercury, 24 February 2005, front page) on an earthquake that hit Southern Africa the day before.

HUGE QUAKE SOWS PANIC

Shocks felt far and wide

The second strongest earthquake to hit Southern Africa in 100 years killed two people in Mozambique yesterday and across the region strong after-shocks sent frightened residents into the streets.

The magnitude 7.5 earthquake was felt in areas as far-flung as Durban and Johannesburg, and also in towns in Zimbabwe and Zambia. Mozambican President Armando Guebuza appealed for calm and asked people to return to their normal lives.

Danny Naidoo, duty manager at the Tropicana Hotel on Durban's beachfront, said he was on the ninth floor when he felt the building sway. "It was quite scary, and at the time I thought the building would collapse," he said.

Glen Dorrofield, duty manager at the Blue Waters Hotel, said he was cashing up the bar when he saw the lights swinging and felt the tremor. It lasted a couple of minutes but Dorrofield said he only realised what was happening when guests started complaining and he noticed the residents from the flat opposite the hotel, running out into the streets.

A resident of Belmont Flats said she had been in bed when she felt the bed rocking. Mabuyi Dlamini, a street vendor who was asleep at the site of his stall at the time of the tremor, said he had been awakened suddenly and noticed screaming people running out of the Balmoral Hotel.

Marie Venter of Oresbury said that her parrot, Sha-sha-lee, had woken her with a shriek: "She was so scared and I tried to calm her down. Animals are very sensitive". Other pet owners reported that their dogs dived under beds and that cats were distressed.

For discussion

How would you cope with the above situation?

Remember that such a natural disaster happens suddenly, without warning.

Which Ubuntu life-coping skills could apply in a situation like this?

THE WISDOM OF UBUNTU

INTRODUCTION

In the foregoing chapter the traditional beliefs or guidelines for wise living were exposed. The challenge is to apply these truths and wisdoms in everyday life.

You only live once. Senior citizens often cannot believe that their lives are almost at an end: Time flies at an amazing speed.

It is therefore wise to enjoy every moment of life.

TO PONDER ON

Uhuru Phalafala's extended family lives in a remote part of the Limpopo Province of South Africa.
The people are completely isolated from urban and developed towns, and you can only reach the area on foot. Most inhabitants have never seen a white person.

The extended family live off the land, eating mostly wild vegetables like marogo (spinach), fruits like marula, tree fruit and pap (stiff porridge made from mealie meal). Alcohol is produced from sorghum ingredients.

Cows are only slaughtered at certain ritual events or celebrations, which are preceded by communication procedures with the specific cow and ancestors, during which the reasons for the slaughter are explained in detail.

The tribe lives in accordance with ancient traditional Ubuntu living and life values, and due to its complete geographical isolation from the outside world (they have no shops, TV, cars or even radios!) the tribe has not been influenced by any values of any other culture. Uhuru, due to the caring attitudes of some outsiders, was one of the first to be educated in tertiary institutions in the outside world of "white people".

These values or beliefs are encapsulated in the following poem by Uhuru, who was only one of few young members of the extended family to receive an education in Polokwane, a "developed" town. For an income she plays the African drum at celebrations and social events.

This poem was published (2004:18) when Uhuru was still in her early 20s.

LIVE FOR NOW

Live for now
Seize the day
Treasure the present
For you are living in it
Tomorrow will come to the world
But not guaranteed to your life
Fear not death because it is inevitable
Rather try and achieve it happy
Life is given and taken back
So appreciate it while you have it
Go all out, be grateful for it
Laugh, and take advantage of today
Where and when else are you gonna do it?

You only live once
When you wake up alive
You should celebrate
Dwell in life rather than death
If you lurk in the shadows of death
You'll live in a cold, dark cloud
You'll focus more on what you don☐t have
You'll conceive life as miserable
So live for now
Love life and life will love you
Many birthdays lead to your death
But you celebrate them
So why not just celebrate life?
Untame your spirit, live happily.

As a well-known saying advises:

Love the life you live, live the life you love.

PERSONAL EXERCISE: LIVING UBUNTU VALUES

Seclude yourself in a quiet and peaceful environment which is conducive to intense and concentrated thinking.

Focus on the personal application of the Ubuntu values, coping skills and outcomes. Outcomes are the end products of the exercise, which are informed by someone's ability to cope with life as a result of learning about Ubuntu. Outcomes are related to the achievement of mastering life-coping skills, which can benefit your personal environment and even your community.

An outcome (in a psychological sense) is described (Bellis, 2000:54) as the realised vision in the development of a person.

On your own, brainstorm your understanding of the following Ubuntu values (as highlighted in the preceding chapter) which guide a happy personality. For reference purposes the appropriate isiZulu word is also provided.

Ubuntu personality values include

➤ togetherness (umoya)
➤ brotherhood (ubuzalwane)
➤ equality (ukulingana)
➤ sharing (isabelo)
➤ sympathy (isisa)
➤ empathy (uzwela)
➤ compassion (umunyu)
➤ respect (ukuhlonipha)
➤ tolerance (yeka)
➤ humanness (ubuntu)
➤ harmony (ubungane)
➤ redistribution (ukwabelwa)
➤ obedience (ukulalela)
➤ happiness (singcolile)
➤ wisdom (ubudoda).

Ubuntu life-coping skills manifest in people

➤ facilitating togetherness
➤ implementing brotherhood
➤ supporting equality

➤ endorsing sharing

➤ expressing sympathy

➤ practising empathy

➤ honouring compassion

➤ maintaining respect

➤ allowing tolerance

➤ saluting humanness

➤ propagating harmony

➤ redistributing wealth (and knowledge)

➤ applying obedience

➤ living happiness

➤ loving wisdom.

You may wonder about the outcomes when practicing these skills. How will they impact on your life?

Ubuntu life-coping skills outcomes allow you to

➤ facilitate togetherness by improving teamwork, the family atmosphere, giving moral support

➤ implement brotherhood so bring about unity, simunye (we are one), solidarity, commitment

➤ support equality by practising non-discrimination, acceptance by all

➤ endorse sharing, creating different responsibilities, bringing happiness and allowing you to participate in the sorrow of others

➤ show sympathy by applied listening, problem analysis, giving consolation

➤ practise empathy through established open-mindedness, understanding

➤ honour compassion, which leads you to value peace, cohesion, warmth

➤ show respect by honouring structured order, discipline, dignity

➢ allow tolerance through self-controlled calmness, level-headedness, forgiveness

➢ salute humanness by exhibiting gentleness, bliss-ness, helpfulness

➢ propagate harmony which results in steadiness, non-chaos, a clarity of vision

➢ redistribute wealth (and knowledge) which leads to sustainability, cooperation, capacity-building, empowerment

➢ apply obedience: justified relationship, convention, custom, values, norms

➢ live happiness which manifests as enjoyed spontaneity, longevity and friendliness

➢ love wisdom which is seen in your resolve, decision-making ability, ability to evaluate, and happiness.

Lastly, flowing from all the above Ubuntu lessons and skills, the main secrets of good life are simple:

Have fun
Just be happy
Be

BIBLIOGRAPHY

Asmal, K. 2002. *Letter to author.* Tshwane: Ministry of National Education.

Battion, R. 2005. *A practical guide for people with life challenges, disorders and their caregivers.* Wright State University: Crown House Publishing.

Beeld Newspaper. 16 March 2006. Jo'burg: National Press.

Bellis, I. 2000. *Skills development.* Johannesburg: Knowledge Resources.

Bhengu, M.J. 1996. *Ubuntu: The essence of democracy.* Cape Town: Novalis Press.

Biko, S. 1978. *I write what I like.* London: Heinemann.

Bremer, S.N. 1980. *How to get what you want.* New York: Success Enterprises

Broodryk, J. 1995. Interview with Sages: Research paper. Tshwane: Ubuntu School of Philosophy

Broodryk, J. 1997. *Ubuntuism as a world view to order society.* D Litt thesis. Tshwane: University of South Africa.

Broodryk, J. 2002. *Ubuntu: Life lessons from Africa.* Tshwane: Ubuntu School of Philosophy.

Broodryk, J. 2005. *Ubuntu management philosophy.* Johannesburg: Knowledge Resources

Broodryk, J. 2006. *The challenge of Ubuntu education today.* Paper delivered at international Education Conference: Bela-Bela: Ubuntu School of Philosophy

Carnegie, D. 1936 (and later editions). *How to win friends and influence people.* New York: Publisher unknown.

Chinkanda, N.E. 1990. *Shared values and Ubuntu.* Unpublished paper. Tshwane: Kontak Conference, HSRC.

Christie, P, Lessen R, & Mbigi L. 1994. *African management.* Johannesburg: Knowledge Resources.

Diescho, J. 1993. *Ubuntu.* Paper delivered at students' conference. Tshwane: University of South Africa.

Du Preez, H. 1997. *Meet the rainbow nation.* Pretoria: Kagiso Tertiary.

Frost, P.J. 2003. *Toxic emotions at work.* Massachusets: Harvard Business School.

Harvard Business Essentials. 2004a. *Manager's toolkit.* Massachussets: Harvard Business School Press.

Harvard Business Essentials. 2004b. *Crisis management.* Massachussets: Harvard Business School Press.

Hountondji, P. 1999. *The particular, the universal.* Article in SAPINA. Vol 2, no. 2. Stanford University Press.

Infomax 3. 1994. Newsletter. Tshwane: Ubuntu Centre.

Jossey-Bass series. 2005. San Francisco: Jossey-Bass. **what series??**

Katholi, G. 1997. *Making caring your target.* Mombay: Better Yourself Books.

Khoza, R.J. 1994. *Ubuntu as African humanism.* Johannesburg: Unpublished draft paper.

Koka, KD. 1996a. *The African renaissance.* Paper delivered. Pretoria: Ubuntu School of Philosophy.

Koka, K.D. 1996b. Sage Philosophy. *The significance of Ubuntu Philosophy*. Johannesburg: Pan-African symposium.

Koka, KD. 1999. *Ubuntu: A peoples' humanness*. Paper delivered. Pretoria: Ubuntu School of Philosophy.

Koka, KD. 2002. *Afrikology* (motivation). The Study of Africa. Unpublished paper. Johannesburg: Gauteng Social Services.

Lenaka, J.1995. *Some misconceptions about cultural differences*. Unpublished paper. Tshwane: Ubuntu School of Philosophy.

Leslau, C & Leslau, W. 1985. *African proverbs*. New York: Peter Pauper Press.

Lesole, I. 2002. *Moral Regeneration*. Unpublished paper delivered at youth workshop. Johannesburg: Gauteng Department of Social Services.

Losyk, B. 2005. *Get a grip!* New Jersey: John Wiley & Sons.

Louw, D.J. *Ubuntu and religion*. Unpublished paper. Polokwane: Ubuntu School of Philosophy.

Lucas, R.W. 1994. *Effective interpersonal relationships*. New York: McGraw-Hill.

Luthuli, A, Kaunda, K, Chisiza, D, Mboya, T, & Nyerere, K.K. 1964. *Africa's freedom*. London: Unwin Books.

Makhudu, N. August 1993. *Cultivating a climate of co-operation through Ubuntu*. Johannesburg: Enterprise magazine.

Malimbe, R.M. 1997. *Child abuse in seSotho folktale*s. Unpublished paper. Tshwane: Ubuntu School of Philosophy.

Mandela, N.R. 1994. *Long walk to freedom*. Randburg: MacDonald Purnell.

Mangani, N.C. 1983. *Exiles and homecoming*. A bibliography of Es'kia Mphalele. Johannesburg: Raven Press.

Mann, S. 2004. *Anger management*. London: Hodder & Stoughton.

Mbigi, L, & Maree, J. 1995. *Ubuntu: the spirit of African transformation management*. Johannesburg: Knowledge Resources.

Mbigi, L.1997. *Ubuntu: The African dream in management*. Johannesburg: Knowledge Resources.

Mbiti, J.J. 1996. *African religion and philosophy*. London: Heineman.

Mdluli, F. 1987. *Ubuntu-Botho*. Inkatha's People Education. Johannesburg: Transformation 5.

Mfenyana, B. February 1986. *Ubuntu article*. Johannesburg: Sash Magazine.

Mokiti, F.K. 1988. *Ujamaa socialism and African religious heritage*. Rome: Pontifical Gregorian University.

Moodie, R. 1960. *Article on Stavenisse shipwreck*. Cape Town: The Record.

Motshekga, M.1988. *The ideology behind witchcraft and the principle of fraud in Criminal Law, in J. Hund (ed)*. Law and statistics in South Africa. Johannesburg: Institute for Public Interest Law and Research.

Mutahhari, A.M. 1995. *The limits of science*. (in Presbey, G.M, Struhl, K.J, and Olsen, R.E. The Philosophical Quest). New York: McGraw-Hill.

Mutwa, C. 1966. *Indaba my children*. London: Kahn & Averaill.

Mutwa, C. 1997. *Usiko. Tales from Africa's treasure trove*. Johannesburg: Telkom.

Mwakabana, H.A.O. 2002. Religious papers. Lutheran World Association: Geneva

Ndaba, J. 1995. Interview on Ubuntu world view. Zululand: Ubuntu School of Philosophy.

Nemavhandu, M. 2002. *Intellectual fraud and its impact on Human Development.* Unpublished paper. Pretoria: Kara Heritage Institute.

Odera Oruka, H. 1991. Sage philosophy. Nairobi: Acts Press.

Odera Oruka, H. 1992. *Oginga Odinga. His philosophy and beliefs.* Nairobi: Initiatives Publishers:

Oduro, G.K. 2006. *Role modelling and communal values.* Paper delivered at International Education Conference on Ubuntu. Bela-Bela: EMASA.

Parrinder, G.1967. *African mythology.* London: Paul Hymden.

Parrott, L.1987. *The habit of happiness.* Waco: Word Books

Phalafala, Uhuru. 2004. *Raisibe: My analogy of freedom.* Polokwane: Ebenhezer.

Presbey, G. 1995. *African Sage philosophers in action*: Essence. Vol 1. No 1. Lagos: Department of Philosophy: University of Lagos.

Presbey, G. 1996. *Ways in which oral philosophy is superior to written philosophy.* Unpublished Paper. Poughkeepsie: Marist College.

Presbey, G.M, Struhl, K.J, & Olsen,J. 2002. *The philosophical quest.* New York: McGraw-Hill.

Presbey, G. 1997. *The wisdom of African sages.* Unpublished paper. Poughkeepsie: Marist College.

Prinsloo, E.D. 1999. *The Ubuntu concept of caring.* Pretoria: Unpublished paper. Tshwane: Ubuntu School of Philosophy.

Ramose, M.B. 1999. *African philosophy through Ubuntu*. Harare: Mondi Books.

Rogers, C. 1995. *On becoming a person: A therapist's view of psychotherapy*. New York: Houghton Mifflin.

Savory, P. 1988. *The best of African folklore*. Cape Town: Struik Publishers.

Senghor, L.S. 1965. *Prose and poetry*. Oxford University Press.

Shutte, A. 2001. *Ubuntu. An ethic for a new South Africa*. Pietermaritzburg: Cluster Publications.

Sindane, J.P.1994. *Democracy and political tolerance*. Unpublished Paper. Tshwane: Ubuntu School of Philosophy.

Sisulu W. 1993. *Ubuntu interview*. Johannesburg: Unpublished.

Sparks, A. 1990. *The mind of South Africa*. London: Heinemann.

Stone, F.M. 2003. *Manager's question and answer book*. New York: Amacom.

Teffo, L.J. 1998. *Ethics in African humanism*. Pretoria: Ubuntu School of Philosophy.

Tintinger, L.A. 1999. *Cries without tears*. Craighall: Corrective Action Holdings.

Van der Wal, H. 2005. *How to facilitate and assess a life skills learning programme*. Johannesburg: Knowledge Resources

Vilikaze, HW. 1991. *The roots of Ubuntu/Botho*. Midrand: Paper delivered at SECOSAF seminar.

INDEX

A

Abantu – 22, 24
Action programme – 138, 144, 145, 153
Advisors – 153, 179
African languages – 23
African pub – 156
African three-legged pot – 151
Alcoholic-to-be – 145
Analogy of the african pot – 149
Ancient holy belief of maat (Ubuntu) – 6
Apartheid era – 126
Application of Ubuntu in practical life – 131
Appreciation – 14, 21, 33, 72, 73, 74, 75,
    81, 104, 105, 106, 107, 113, 162,
    171, 172

B

Baba – 52
Background – 4, 135
Batho pele – 25
Botho – 21, 23, 24, 174, 175
Bunhu – 24

C

Caring – 3, 14, 22, 25, 27, 28, 42-46, 48,
    50, 52, 53, 77, 109, 121, 131, 133,
    136, 141, 143, 153, 157, 171, 173,
    175
Case study – 16, 29, 40, 51, 61, 74, 75,
    86, 93, 106, 107, 118, 131, 133, 146,
    192
Caution – 159
Charity – 22, 30, 50
Children's rights – 14, 35, 74, 106
Cohesion – 15, 22, 28, 82, 86, 114, 118,
    165, 199
Commitment – 14, 18, 19, 28, 67, 78, 82,
    99, 110, 114, 165, 173, 186, 187, 199
Compassion
    -   about emotion – 77, 109
    -   associated values – 22

-   each other – 79, 111
-   examples – 79, 111
-   for others – 81, 113
-   honour – 198, 199
-   integrates – 110
-   influences – 15
-   life of Africans – 79, 111
-   people – 77, 109
-   reaching out – 78, 110
-   relates – 78, 110
-   respect – 79, 111
-   to children – 81, 86, 113, 118
-   values – 86, 118
-   vital – 15
Consideration – 19, 21, 63, 73, 75, 95,
    105, 107, 121, 139, 177,
Counselling – 3, 16, 18, 134, 135, 142,
    149-154, 156, 157, 168, 173
Cultural differences – 79, 111

D

Definitions – 13, 14, 17, 19
Democratic – 39, 128, 178
Developing – 144, 154, 157
Dignity – 14, 21, 22, 28, 35, 67, 68, 78,
    99, 100, 110, 130, 157, 166, 199

E

Earthquake – 192, 193
Echo of life – 51
Empathy – 28, 38, 47, 48, 73, 78, 105,
    110, 157, 172, 185, 198, 199
Exercise – 12, 16, 51, 53, 54, 134, 136,
    145, 146, 152, 154, 176, 182, 191, 197

F

Family
    -   atmosphere – 165, 186, 199
    -   extended – 12, 14, 21, 33, 46, 65,
            69, 79, 97, 101, 111, 120,
            121, 165, 174, 176, 177, 185,
            186, 195, 196

- live – 195
- members – 46, 57, 65, 89, 97, 143
- structures – 21
- forms – 46
- issues – 37
- systems – 69. 101

Familyhood – 23
Forgiveness – 15, 25, 28, 83, 86, 115, 118, 128, 199
Formulating – 137, 141, 150
Friendliness – 28, 50, 200

G

Greed – 59, 60, 61, 73, 91, 92, 93, 105, 162, 184, 189
Greedy poultry farmer – 61, 93

H

Happiness – 16, 17, 18, 27, 28, 49, 81, 113, 135, 150, 159, 169, 184, 188, 189, 190, 191, 198, 199, 200
Harmonious – 3, 33, 44, 52, 59, 68, 69, 91, 100, 101, 156, 161, 181, 182, 183
Helpfulness – 28, 49, 199
Historical – 4, 11, 27, 34
Human rights – 3, 14, 25, 32, 33, 34, 35
Humanity – 14, 22, 28, 31, 32, 39, 40, 41, 121

I

Implementing Ubuntu – 3
Indunas – 179
Influence of maat – 9
Informality – 15, 28, 80, 83, 112, 115

K

Kindness – 15, 31, 41, 85, 86, 117, 118, 183, 186, 190

l

Life lessons – 1-3, 13, 66, 84, 98, 116, 160, 188
Lobola issue – 74, 106

M

Mahala – 55, 87

Medicine – 4, 36
Mensheid – 24
Menslikgeit – 24
Methodology – 15, 122, 135, 136, 136, 137, 155
Methology – 151
Modern living – 122, 126
Motho – 174

N

Ngabantu – 77, 109
Ninjane – 78, 110
Norms – 14, 26, 32, 65, 69, 70, 71, 97, 101, 102, 103, 185, 200
Ntate – 45, 77, 109
Numunhu – 23
Nunhu – 24

O

Obedience – 14, 28, 63, 68, 80, 95, 100, 112, 186, 187, 199, 200
ONPO analysis – 15, 16, 138, 142, 144, 146, 150, 153, 156
Open-handedness – 14, 60, 92, 167

P

Peace – 14, 28, 39, 40, 49, 65, 81, 97, 113, 128, 130, 179, 181, 184, 190, 191, 199
Perceptions – 17, 19, 20, 21, 23, 25, 27, 29, 47, 157
Personal action plan – 138, 144
Personal exercise – 197
Personal mission – 141
Personal vision – 15, 141
Philosophy – 4, 9, 16, 21, 25, 27, 122, 136, 142, 143, 144, 153, 154, 159, 159, 165, 183, 184, 188, 189, 191
Pitseng – 16, 149, 151, 152, 157
Poem – 12, 196
Practical living – 119, 121, 123, 125, 127, 129, 131, 131
Problematic issue – 138
Prominence of Ubuntu – 24, 25
Pungwe – 176

R

Redistribution – 14, 28, 59, 60, 91, 92, 184, 185, 198

Regeneration – 26, 129, 130, 144, 171
Religion – 4, 9, 10, 25, 31, 33, 36, 39, 71, 72, 81, 82, 103, 104, 113, 114, 155, 175, 176, 185, 190, 192
Religiosity – 71, 72, 103, 104
Robben island experience – 40
Role – 4, 40, 46, 47, 64, 96, 122, 123, 153, 155, 156, 181, 188
Rules – 26, 63, 69, 70, 71, 95, 101, 102, 103, 130, 175, 180, 186, 187

S

Sangoma – 16, 72, 80, 104, 112, 126, 135,   153, 156, 173
Self-motivation – 15, 67, 99, 133, 134, 135, 136, 137, 139, 141, 143, 145, 147
SeSotho – 23, 45
Shangaan – 23
Shebeen – 57, 89, 156
Shona – 24
Simunye – 164, 199
Solidarity – 22, 164, 199
Spirit of oneness – 165
Spiritual – 22, 31, 48, 72, 82, 104, 114, 126, 167, 175, 189, 190
Spontaneity – 15, 28, 80, 84, 86, 112, 116, 118, 200
Story of an artist – 146
Surviving – 192
Swahili – 24, 51
Sympathy – 28, 48, 49, 157, 167, 169, 198, 199

T

Taxi violence – 29
Teamwork – 82, 114, 164, 187, 199
Togetherness – 23, 163, 169, 198, 199
Tolerance – 14, 28, 34, 35, 36, 128, 176, 181, 198, 199
Traditional life – 119
Tribes – 123, 137, 165, 185
Tsonga – 24

U

Ubuntu personality – 16, 161, 162, 184, 198
Ubuntu skills – 16, 159, 163
Ubuntu values – 34, 118, 121, 129, 143, 144, 161, 165, 166, 197

Ujamaa – 24
Ukuhlonipha – 63, 95, 198
Umoja – 163
Unconditionally – 14, 50, 59, 91
Understanding – 6, 14, 19, 21, 22, 28, 32, 34, 38, 38, 47, 126, 134, 136, 140, 146, 155, 156, 173, 179, 185, 197, 199
Unhu – 23, 24
Utu – 24, 51

V

Value of caring – 14, 43
Value of compassion – 77
Value of humanness – 14, 51
Value of respect – 14, 63, 64, 95, 96
Value of sharing - 14, 55, 60, 87, 92,
Vhuthu – 23

W

Wisdom – 2, 10, 16, 65, 102, 122, 127, 131, 136, 149, 155-157, 163, 165-168
Work celebration – 118
World view of Ubuntu – 1, 3, 5, 7, 9, 11, 13, 15

X

Xhosa – 22, 50, 69, 87

Z

Zulu – 132, 154

GLOSSARY

Abantu	Ugandan term for Ubuntu, also described as a fellowship of tribes.
Baba	Sign of respect towards an old man.
Batho pele	People first.
Bohadi	A Sesotho word for lobola.
Botho or Motho	A Sesotho term for Ubuntu.
Braai	Barbeque facility.
Braaivleis	Barbequed meat.
Bunhu	A Tsonga term for Ubuntu.
Dolos	Art of throwing the bones, of divination.
Dumela	Not only a way of greeting a person, but also an enquiry as to the other person's friends and relatives.
Ex Africa semper aliquid novi	Out of Africa always something new.
Go ya ka magoro gase go tswane melato re a rerisana	Even if we may go our own way, whenever urgent and vital issues arise, we still have the obligation to come together and to try to find a common solution to these issues.
Ilima	Harmonious exchange, helping another.
Llobolo	A Zulu word for lobola.
Imbizo	Bush meetings – meetings of a mass congregation or public, which is broader and on a national level.
Indaba	Open discussion by a group of people who share the same interests.
Indunas	Advisors.
Kratia	Rule or authority.
Lapa	Social hut.

Lekgotla	A meeting lasting hours, which takes place at a secluded venue.
Lobola	A social system and custom in terms of which a bridegroom donates bride's gifts in the form of a number of cattle to the family-in-law.
Mahala	An African concept that says that it is fine to give something to others free of charge, without expecting something in return.
Mama	Sign of respect towards an old woman.
Mensheid	Afrikaans term for Ubuntu.
Menslikgeit	Cape Afrikaans term for Ubuntu.
Motho	Tswana term for Ubuntu.
Mukwerera	Production festival ceremony.
Munhu munhu	Implies that man is entitled to unconditional respect, dignity, acceptance, and care from his significant relevant group or community.
Muti	Medicine.
Ninjane	How are all of you?
Ntate	A Sesotho word to address an old man or respected father figure.
Numunhu or munhu	A Shangaan term for Ubuntu.
Nyanga	Herbalist or diviner.
Nyarwath	Corruption.
Pungwe	Work celebration.
Sangoma	Spiritual medicine man.
Shebeen	African pub.
Shosholoza	Teamwork in a collective sense.
Simunye	Solidarity.
Simunye	Solidarity or spirit of oneness.
Siza	Zulu word for people-ness (humanness).
Spaza shops	House trading outlets.
Stokvel	Informal cooperative enterprise and economy.

Tokolosh	Bad, devilish-looking little creature.
Tsotsi	Bad person or criminal.
Ubuntu	Zulu concept that means 'personhood', and which is also known as *unhu* in Shona and *botho* in both Tswana and Sotho. Ubuntu is the essence of being human, and is a positive perception of African personhood. It refers to the collective interdependence and solidarity of communities of affection. Ubuntu literally means 'I am because we are, I can only be a person through others'.
Ubuntu or umtu	Zulu term for Ubuntu.
Ubuntu or umuntu	Xhosa term for Ubuntu.
Ujamaa	Tanzanian concept – family-hood. This relates to the concept of universal brotherhood or African socialism.
Ukuhlonipha	Respect in the Zulu language.
Umhlangano	Democratic management practice – desirable that discussion groups or interactive forums be established in a similar manner.
Umoja	Togetherness.
Umuntu ngumuntu ngabantu	I am a person through other human beings.
Unhu or nunhu	Shona term for Ubuntu.
Utu	Swahili term for Ubuntu.
Vhuthu or muthu	Venda term for Ubuntu.

ABBREVIATIONS

BPR   Business Process Re-engineering

CIP   Continuous Improvement Philosophy

JIT   Just in Time Inventory
             Management

MBI   Management By Involvement

MBWA   Managing By Walking Around

MWA   Managing By Walking Around

ONPO   Obstacles, Negatives, Positives,
             Opportunities

PDM   Purpose-directed Management

QSCVM   Quality, Service, Cleanliness, Value

SM   Strategic Management

SWOT   Strengths, Weaknesses, Opportunities,
             Threats

TPM   Total Productivity Management

TQM   Total Quality Management

UMP   Ubuntu Management Philosophy

Addendum Training Programme

Training of ubuntu life coping skills based on the book

DAY ONE

- ➤ Arrival at sunset
- ➤ Registration
- ➤ Handing in arm watches (to experience time-less training)
- ➤ Welcoming
- ➤ Traditional name introduction
- ➤ African name-giving ceremony/baptism
- ➤ Group tribal division: humming ice breaker
- ➤ Booking into kaias (sleeping shack)
- ➤ Traditional African supper (all meals may be enjoyed with hands)
- ➤ Ice breaker: observation exercise
- ➤ Introduction to training course
- ➤ Exercise: farewell to beloved ones
- ➤ Uninhibited laughing competition

DAY TWO

- ➤ Wake up call at sunrise
- ➤ Rise and shine
- ➤ Exploring Sizanani Training Center on foot

➢   Traditional breakfast
➢   Empathy: a caring practical experience
    (interact with mentally and physical disabled children)

Participative training:

➢   The Ubuntu worldview
➢   Case study: being captive in a taxi war
➢   Refreshments
➢   The value of HUMANNESS
➢   Case study: the Robben Island experience
➢   The value of CARING
➢   Case study: the echo of life
➢   The value of SHARING
➢   Case study: is it theft to steal from an exploitive employer?
➢   The value of RESPECT
➢   Case study: is lobola (bridesgift convention) permissible in
    terms of Ubuntu?
➢   Lunch
➢   Ice breaker: mirror personalities
➢   The value of COMPASSION
➢   Case study: socialising (pungwe)
➢   The PRACTICAL LIVING of Ubuntu values
➢   Case study: universal application of values
➢   Ubuntu self-motivation
➢   Exercise: alcoholic-to-be
➢   Case study: story of an artist
➢   Relaxation, swimming, footing, sitting around
➢   Sunset experience in park: traditional self-braai
➢   Pungwe: African social event

DAY THREE

➢   Ubuntu meditation experience at sunrise
➢   Fruit breakfast

Participative training:

➢ Ubuntu counselling process
➢ Case study: Analogy of the African pot (Pitseng)
➢ Ubuntu LIFE COPING skills
➢ Refreshments
➢ Exercise: PERSONAL IMPLEMENTATION of Ubuntu life coping skills
➢ Case study: Coping with an earthquake
➢ Certificates
➢ Handing back watches
➢ Lunch

➢ Indaba (discussion/evaluation) about training and experiences
➢ Hamba Kahle/Thaila (go well departure time)

Man does not always practise a basic and simple truth of successful life, namely that Man was given the serenity

➢ *to change the things Man can change,*
➢ *to accept the things Man cannot change and*
➢ *the wisdom to distinguish between the two.*

Knowres publishing publications

Knowres Publishing is a company that was established under the Knowledge Resources umbrella.

We focus on the world of work, business and organisations, as we believe these are important elements in many people's lives.

Knowres Publishing is committed to offering products that will enhance and facilitate skill building and the development of potential. Products are carefully selected to provide value to organisations, employees and of the individual.

See next pages for our latest publications.

Johannesburg Office:
The Mews, Oxford Road, Rosebank
P O Box 3954, Randburg, 2125
Tel. No. (011) 880-8540
Fax. No. (011) 880-8700
E-mail: cia@knowres.co.za

Cape Town Office:
1st Floor, Sterling Place, 86 Edward Street,
Tygervalley, Bellville, 7530
Tel. No. (021) 919-7685
Fax. No. (021) 919-7704
E-mail: knowresct@knowres.co.za

Visit our website www.kr.co.za for more information

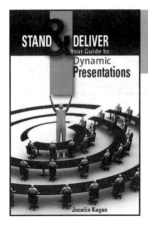

STAND & DELIVER
Your guide to dynamic presentations

Jocelin Kagan

R189.00   ISBN 1-86922-137-0

STAND & DELIVER is written especially for you, the **business person** striving forward in your career. This is no ordinary step by step "how to do presentations" book. It is special.

Jocelin uses the most recent neuroscientific findings to acquaint you with the intimate workings of your brain. The **plus factor** is that it shows you how to **strengthen**, **stimulate**, and **exercise** your whole brain while gaining **confidence**, **mental clarity,** and **verbal fluency**. It will show you how to present yourself in the most appealing manner.

Personal Balanced Scorecard
The way to individual happiness, personal integrity, and organisational effectiveness

R189.00   ISBN: 1-86922-141-9

This publication offers a new holistic management concept which includes a search for self-knowledge and self-discovery. By routinely applying the complete PBSC method, self-knowledge will be transformed into wisdom. The result of using this method is a continuous voyage to greater happiness, personal growth, and freedom.
The contents include:

PART I: PBSC as an instrument for individual development, personal effectiveness and
growth in life – The Personal Balanced Scorecard, implementing the Personal Balanced Scorecard, aligning personal ambition with personal behaviour and personal integrity

PART II: PBSC as an instrument for enjoyment and effective talent development at work – aligning personal ambition with shared ambition, aligning personal and shared ambition with business ethics, shared integrity, rolling out the Balanced Scorecards, effective talent management, The PBSC cycle

SKILLS DEVELOPMENT PRACTICE MADE EASY
Education Training and Development Guidelines and Resources
Elaine Folscher and Linda Chonco

Price: R799.00
ISBN1-86922-136-2 (Loose-leaf format)

This handbook offers skills development facilitators a comprehensive resource on dealing with skills development imperatives such as job competence development, affirmative action, succession planning and broad-based black economic empowerment.

Included in this work is a handy reference of standard occupational levels and categories as well as definitions, abbreviations and acronyms which are vital to anyone involved in the field of human capital development in South Africa.

There are over 100 Internet links to a toolkit of guidelines and resources for the skills development practitioner, available from: **www.kr.co.za/ Skills Development Templates.htm**

A FRAMEWORK FOR THE DEVELOPMENT OF LEARNING PROGRAMMES FOR ADULT LEARNERS IN OUTCOMES-BASED MODE
Ursula Moodie and co-author Sarah Gravett

Price: R799.00
ISBN 1-86922-138-9 (Loose-leaf format)

A framework for the development of fearning programmes for adult learners in outcomes-based mode systematically guides programme planners and educators in planning and designing outcomes-based learning programmes.

The diagrammatic representation of events at the start of each chapter assists in planning and designing the learning programme. The purpose, expected outcomes and preamble are outlined, and the accompanying list of theoretical underpinnings and critical cross-field outcomes makes for easy referencing.

FUNDAMENTALS FOR EFFECTIVE MENTORING
Raising giant killers

Niël Steinmann

R249.00   ISBN: 1-86922-140-0

Niël Steinmann's unique book draws on the life of the lioness, the queen of the African bush. *Raising Giant Killers* shares the wonderful analogy of the lioness and how she prepares her cubs for (and raises them in) an extremely harsh and ruthless world. Her ability to make time, care for, nurture, protect, teach, expose and eventually wean her cubs to become "giant killers" is truly remarkable. **The survival and competence of her cubs represent success in the fascinating life cycle of nature – ultimately, their success ensures the future and sustainability of the pride.**

LEVERAGING KNOWLEDGE-BASED ASSETS:
The new value equation to create competitive advantage

R249.00   ISBN: 1-86922-139-7

The approach the authors take is primarily a **pragmatic** and **practical** one with due consideration of the theoretical constructs (albeit sometimes diverse and conflicting) that underlie the main theme of this book – *Leveraging knowledge-based assets: The new value equation to create competitive advantages.*

This book is written for the following practitioners who seek different, innovative, and integrated views on the subject of value creation through knowledge assets:

* Business leaders of knowledge-intensive firms
* Human resource professionals
* Organisation development consultants
* Organisation strategists and change experts
* The inquisitive accountant

The Spirit of African Leadership

Lovemore Mbigi

THE SPIRIT OF AFRICAN LEADERSHIP
Prof Lovemore Mbigi

Price: R189.00   ISBN: 1-86922-127-3

In *The Spirit of African Leadership*, Professor Mbigi investigates the wealth of leadership knowledge that Africa has to share with the global community. Building on a culture with centuries of indigenous knowledge, Professor Mbigi develops coherent and practical leadership frameworks and principles that will help leaders to nurture the emotional, spiritual and cultural resources of their organisations.

UBUNTU
Management Philosophy

Johann Broodryk

UBUNTU: Management Philosophy – Exporting ancient African Wisdom into the Global World

Price: R189.00   ISBN: 1-86922-132-X

Ubuntu Management Philosophy (UMP) has already been applied with great success by various role players in both the private and public sectors in South Africa. In the book, managers are challenged to implement Ubuntu Management Philosophy for improved staff performance, higher productivity and excellent service delivery.

The book focuses on:

* The African concept of ubuntu
* Ubuntu versus conventional management
* Ubuntu and management
* The Ubuntu personality and environment
* Ubuntu cultural concepts
* Ubuntu strategy and marketing
* Ubuntu management guidelines and practices.

UBUNTU: The Spirit of African Transformation Management

Lovemore Mbigi with Jenny Maree

Price: R139.00   ISBN: 1-86922-133-8

It is time modern management put rituals and ceremony as well as spirit, music and dance at the centre and crafted these vital elements into our training and development programmes. *Masibambane* – let us hold together feelings and collective spirit. Let Ubuntu be our premium cultural business and product emblem.

Be INSPIRED or Get EXPIRED

Dr John Tibane
Best-selling author of Do it ... because you can!

Price: R159.00   ISBN: 1-86922-124-9

Your competitive future depends on how capable you are of maximising human capital. Inspiration prepares people for development and makes them participate in their own growth.

Over the course of sections on the PHILOSOPHY, PSALMS, PROVERBS, PARADIGMS, PRACTICES and PROCESS of inspiration, you will be armed with the understanding and skills you need to inspire yourself and others. With this book you are on track to inherit the earth!

DO IT... BECAUSE YOU CAN! THE 21ST CENTURY COMES WITH MORE CHALLENGES THAN PROMISES

Dr John Tibane

R129-00   ISBN: 1-919919-19-8

Dr John Tibane is a management and leadership consultant. His corporation Tibane Consulting specialises in maximising human capital. He is well known for his insights on leadership, potential development, service excellence and productivity.

CONVERSATIONS IN LEADERSHIP: SOUTH AFRICAN PERSPECTIVES

Terry N.A. Meyer and Italia Boninelli

R259.00   ISBN: 1-86922-058-7

The genesis of this book lies in dozens of conversations which occurred between the editors and leaders in various major organisations: The editors have chosen three major themes for this book:

1. There is a discussion about the nature of leadership itself, including interviews with a number of leading thinkers on the subject.
2. Many of the key issues in leadership are explored.
3. The processes involved in growing leaders are explored, with some best practice case studies.

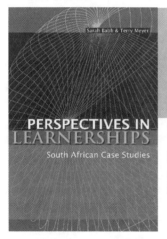

PERSPECTIVES IN LEARNERSHIPS: SOUTH AFRICAN CASE STUDIES

Sarah Babb & Terry Meyer

R259.00   ISBN: 1-86922-132-X

From the contributions to this book the elements of an effective learnership system can be identified. These include the following:

* The overall purpose, aims and objectives of the system
* The governance of the system
* The learning outcomes expressed as a qualification as well as broad individual and corporate objectives
* The selection of the learners
* The quality of learning provision and on-the-job learning and work placement
* The provision of mentoring and coaching support
* The culture of the organisation
* The assessment process, ongoing evaluation and administration of the system.

MENTORING AND COACHING: TOOLS AND TECHNIQUES FOR IMPLEMENTATION

Marius Meyer & Leon Fourie

R279.00   ISBN: 1-86922-056-0

Mentoring and Coaching is the ultimate South African handbook for becoming a world-class mentor and coach. Firmly rooted in the South African context it provides tried, tested and benchmarked guidelines for managers, team leaders, facilitators, mentors or coaches who are required to do some form of mentoring and coaching as part of their job.

Case studies, examples, checklists, evaluation, agreement and self-assessment forms, role-plays, plans and toolboxes are there to help you to

* assess your organisation's mentoring programme
* deal with the pitfalls of mentoring and the management of diversity in the mentor-mentee relationship.

BUILDING HUMAN CAPITAL: SOUTH AFRICAN PERSPECTIVES

Italia Boninelli and Terry N.A. Meyer

R259.00   ISBN: 1-86922-059-5

This book will provide new insights, inspiration and practical tools to improve the ability to grow the human capital that organisations need to succeed in the 21st century.

The editors have chosen five major themes for this book.

1. A discussion about the nature of the landscape within which HR needs to position itself, including some interviews with a number of leading thinkers on the subject.
2. The key issue of how to's.

SIMPLE SOLUTIONS TO STRATEGIC SUCCESS: THE ONE-PAGE C@PS PLANNING PROCESS
Clive Howe

R179-00   ISBN 1-919919-20-1

Simple Solutions to Strategic Success provides you with a strategic planning process simple enough plan to fit onto a single page. You will find the model incredibly easy to understand and implement. It is imbued with such a strong sense of focus that it will allow you to align every single function and daily activity with the vision of your company. In this way the model has become the ultimate link between strategy and operations.

SIMPLE SOLUTIONS TO BALANCING YOUR LIFE
Clive Howe

R179.00   **ISBN: 1-86922-030-7**

Clive Howe takes you through a structured methodology that will enable you to create your own balanced life plan. It is designed as a working document for you to go through the process of formulating a plan of action for creating life balance.

Following Howe's step-by-step model, you can use the space provided in the book to jot down the way you want to live your life (your mission); the values that guide how you behave; the roles you play in life; your personal balanced scorecard consisting of four main pillars – the 4Ms: mind, metabolism, meaning and memory; and the measures (indicators) to check whether you are on track in achieving the 4M balance. At the end of the book you will be able to map your completed plan on a template and print or download it in a practical, simple format that fits onto a single page.

SIMPLE SOLUTIONS TO EFFECTIVE MARKETING!
Dianne Perrett with Clive Howe

Price: R189.00   ISBN: 1-86922-109-5

In *Simple Solutions to Effective Marketing!* Dianne Perrett provides you with a rapid one-day planning process resulting in a simple, live marketing management tool that will direct you towards your ultimate purpose – that of identifying, attracting and retaining satisfied customers.

MEASURING RETURN ON INVESTMENT IN TRAINING
A Practical Implementation Guide

M Meyer, C Opperman and C Dyrbye

R299.00   ISBN: 1-86922-019-6

This book is intended to help human resource and training managers obtain the necessary knowledge and skills to determine ROI in training programmes. *"Measuring Return on Investment in Training"* provides a systematic and integrated approach to the theory and practice of ROI. It also provides a more holistic understanding of the correct application of ROI measurement in the workplace.

You will learn how to… * Measure Return On Investment (ROI) to determine the value of training for your company * Motivate the use of ROI for the organisation * Apply the steps to measure ROI * Calculate ROI for a training intervention and avoid the pitfalls in ROI measurements * Provide guidelines for the correct calculation of ROI and implement the ROI process in an organisation * Overcome resistance to ROI and compile a ROI report for a company.

ASSESSING HUMAN COMPETENCE
Elaine Saunders

R249-00   ISBN: 1-86922-009-0

Amidst a minefield of challenges and obstacles that surrounds assessment in South Africa, the author comes with clear, coherent guidelines for implementing and under standing competency-based, job-related assessment. Apart from being practical and well tested in the workplace, her model has the advantage of incorporating all the ethics, technology, training and cultural issues without which it is not possible to implement a fair assessment process in a culturally heterogeneous country such as South Africa. The author also provides intelligent, helpful discussions of:

* The polemic surrounding psychometric testing, which can make the most valuable contribution in the measurement of intellectual ability and learning potential. * The role of unions as stakeholders in assessment, which is crucial in the development of transparency in the assessment process. * The importance of defensible ethics in assessment and the need to be selective as regards those whom we identify as assessors. * The role of assessment as a self-development tool.

VIABLE BUSINESS STRATEGIES
A systemic, people-centric approach

Marius Ungerer, Maurits Pretorius
& Johan Herholdt

R259.00   ISBN: 1-86922-144-3

The authors provide breakthrough processes and ideas for developing and implementing strategy. This book is a must-have resource for increasing the thinking capacity and collective intelligence of strategy makers.

It introduces systems thinking to strategic frameworks, and strategy becomes a continuous, dynamic, learning conversation that involves the complex interplay of all the strategic variables in a business.